The Tassajara Bread Book

ALSO BY EDWARD ESPE BROWN

The Complete Tassajara Cookbook

Tassajara Cooking

The Tassajara Recipe Book

The

TASSAJARA
BREAD
BOOK

Edward Espe Brown

S H A M B H A L A
Boston & London
2009

SHAMBHALA PUBLICATIONS, INC.
Horticultural Hall
300 Massachusetts Avenue
Boston, Massachusetts 02115
www.shambhala.com

9 8 7 6 5 4 3 2 1

Printed in the United States of America

⊗ This edition is printed on acid-free paper that meets the
American National Standards Institute z39.48 Standard.
♻ This book was printed on 30% postconsumer recycled paper.
For more information please visit www.shambhala.com.
Distributed in the United States by Random House, Inc.,
and in Canada by Random House of Canada Ltd

The Library of Congress Cataloging-in-Publication Data
Brown, Edward Espe.
The Tassajara bread book/Edward Espe Brown.
p. cm.
Includes index.
ISBN 978-1-59030-704-5
1. Bread. I. Title.
TX769.B83 2009
641.8'15 — dc22
2008044901

Book Design by Steve Dyer

Dedicated
with respect and appreciation
to all my teachers
past, present, and future:
gods, men, and demons;
beings, animate and inanimate,
living and dead, alive and dying.

Rock and water
wind and tree
bread dough rising

Vastly all
are patient with me.

Bread makes itself, by your kindness, with your help, with imagination streaming through you, with dough under hand, you are breadmaking itself, which is why breadmaking is so fulfilling and rewarding.

Recipes do not belong to anyone—given to me, I give them to you. Recipes are only a guide, a skeleton framework, to be fleshed out according to your nature and desire. Your life, your love, will bring these recipes into full creation. This cannot be taught. You already know. So plunge in: cook, love, feel, create. Actualize breadmaking itself.

Contents

Muffins and Quick Breads

Compound Butters

Acknowledgments

In the basement of the Shambhala Bookstore in Berkeley, California, in 1969, Sam Bercholz of Shambhala Publications saw something he liked in a tattered xeroxed manuscript, and said, "I'll give up a $100 advance and 10 percent royalty." Deal. And then he helped conceive many of the original design features: round picture on the cover, brown ink, calligraphy, drawings by Anne Kent Rush and Frances Thompson. The resulting book struck a chord.

This edition, with a new design, new decorative drawings by John David Simpkins (a blessing in my life), and color photos by Patrick Tregenza (what an enjoyable time we had together baking and photoshooting), is the vision of Peter Turner, current president of Shambhala Publications.

Along with inspired publishing, the fact that this book ever came into being is rather incomprehensible and mysterious—who would have thought?

This book first came about as a response to the numerous requests of the students and guests at Tassajara. At their urging, I began to envision what my bread book would be like. In the kitchen we started writing down everything we made. So for the recipes themselves, I would like to acknowledge and thank the following people: Lynn Good, Loring Palmer, Clarke Mason, Alan Winter, Roovan ben Yuhmin, Sandy Hollister, Kobun Chino, Bill Lane, Bob Shuman, Jeff Sherman, Angie Runyon, Maureen or perhaps Madeleine, Connie, Sandy,

Niels Holm, Mary Quagliata, Grandma Dito, and all the other people who have made manifest their love, working in the Beloved Kitchens of Tassajara. (Some of these people have since become Ancestors.)

At times I rather despaired of seeing this book completed. Fortunately the project had the help and encouragement of many people:

I am particularly grateful to Katherine Thanas for her efforts as editor, typist, consultant, proofreader, analyst, and friend, and for her incorrigible good nature. "What does *this* mean?" she would tease. Others who assisted with typing and editing included Alan Marlowe and Diane DiPrima.

Frances Thompson contributed the essential how-to illustrations and Anne Kent Rush did the original decorative drawings.

Members of Zen Center supported me and the process: Peter Schneider, Yvonne Rand, Dick and Virginia Baker, and more recently Michael Wenger and Mel Weitsman.

New to writing I found encouragement from Elizabeth Williams and the Wolfs of Portola Valley.

I will always be grateful to Bob and Anna Beck for getting me started at Tassajara in the summer of 1966, "teaching me everything I know," as Anna puts it.

Lastly, my gratitude and blessings to Jim Vaughn and Ray Hurslander, my original cooking gurus at Tassajara. They shared everything they could. At the time there was no way to know how extraordinary that was.

May we all nourish each other.

Edward Espe Brown
January 2009

Introduction

VISITING MY AUNT ALICE IN FALLS CHURCH, VIRGINIA,
in the summer of 1955, I discovered home-baked bread. "Discovered"
is probably not an adequate word to convey my heavenly joy in the
welcome-home aromas, my intense pleasure in the tasting (with butter
and jam!), and my incredible fulfillment in the eating: something inside felt met, wanted to jump up and down, and said *thank you*. Unlike
so many things in life which leave something to be desired, homemade
bread fed me. So moved, words tumbled out: *I will learn how to make
bread, and teach others how to make bread.* I had a calling. The resulting
Tassajara Bread Book first appeared in 1970.

It was in 1966 that I finally learned to bake bread from Jim Vaughn
and Ray Hurslander at Tassajara Hot Springs, the last summer before it
was bought by the Zen Center of San Francisco and became a meditation center open to guests from May first through Labor Day. Jimmy
and Ray had learned to bake bread from Alan Hooker, a jazz musician
who bottomed out, he said, in Columbus, Ohio, and became a baker —
later he would start the Ranch House Restaurant in Ojai, California,
where he had moved to study with Krishnamurti. The long lineage of
bakers goes back for centuries, as we today share the craft and pass it
on to others.

With Jim and Ray I again discovered home-baked bread, this time
the making of it: wondrous vitality, intimate absorption, disappearing
into the process — breadmaking itself — love at first touch. So I have

wished to share this, the wholesomeness and well being that arises in the making, baking, and eating of bread. What you knead is what you get. Give bread a hand—and your hands will thank you (along with your stomach).

Since *The Tassajara Bread Book* first appeared, many more bakers, many more bakeries, and many more books on bread have appeared. Unbleached white flour and whole wheat flour are on the supermarket shelves. Small changes, maybe, but I am happy and grateful to have played a small part with the writing of this book.

Over the years numerous people have conveyed how much they appreciated this *Bread Book:* made bread for the first time, enjoyed it, felt the mysterious way in which the simple activity of breadmaking was a fulfilling act of mutual creation, a profound expression of caring, of nurturing oneself and others. As one woman put it, she experienced a "silent, hidden, quiet revolution" taking place in the kitchen and her heart. I know I am not a great baker, but a competent and capable one, and I am glad to have shared some of my joy with others, and to have encouraged others to pick up the ingredients and make something. People responded.

We can inspire one another. We can share know-how and encouragement. Kerry Smith in Bloomington, Indiana, started baking from the *Tassajara Bread Book* in 1970, and initially sold homemade bread door-to-door out of the back of his woody station wagon. Soon, along with members of his ashram, he opened a bakery. Three of them, he said, would knead the bread by hand in a huge mixing bowl, until one day a real baker showed up and laughed at what he saw. He couldn't believe it. Show us, they said, and before long they had seven retail stores and a large bakery *plant* with a twenty-four-shelf oven. In 1976 when we started our retail bakery, the Tassajara Bread Bakery, in San Francisco, we had no experience baking in quantity like that. Kerry, Tano, and Swami Chetanananda came from Indiana to advise us. Back and forth the energy, knowledge, and inspiration flow. Thank goodness, we do not have to dream up everything ourselves. Our lives are intimately connected, inextricably bound together. We can work to feed each other.

My friend Fred felt very fortunate to be able to make bread. Some of his love of baking must have carried over to his daughter Jenny, who once said that where food is, God is. Before he opened Bread and Chocolate, his bakery in Larkspur, he worked for a few weeks at the Tassajara Bakery back in 1979 or 1980—a brief apprenticeship, going to work at three or four in the morning, making bread, eating breakfast with the staff.

Get Fred started and his natural exuberance takes over. "Bread," he says, "helps me center, focus, be. It's good to make, good to eat, gives me time to think, because it takes its own time. You cannot rush the bread, cannot manipulate it. Baking bread will help you connect with everything; it may take years, but. . . ." His pontificating doesn't last long, though, as he concludes, "Bread is what I value—in addition to butter and jam!" Laughter follows, and Fred is happy. "Half of America has a copy of your book," he exaggerates. "Your book transmitted how to bake bread, and it enriched people's lives as well. Now there are big commercial bakeries making many different varieties of bread. You helped spawn a rejuvenation."

Later Fred was inspired to become a nurse, and now works in the emergency room at a local Kaiser Hospital. And Jenny sometimes works there with him as she completes nursing school. Bread for the journey. Warm wishes, Fred.

My baker friend Bruce turned fifty several years ago. His marriage had come apart, and he had lost his job in computers in Cleveland. He ended up in Booneville in the Anderson Valley, a small town mostly known for the fact that it is on the way to Mendocino, a Northern California coastal village that has become a weekend getaway destination. His sense of direction got him that far, but he still felt at loose ends, until one Christmas his daughter Diane gave him a handmade bread bowl and a copy of my book. Baking bread restored him.

When I stopped off to visit Bruce and two of his daughters, Diane and Ellen, they showed me the bowl that had changed his life. Made of coils of clay to resemble a coiled snake, this bowl glowed with inner light. Clearly love and devotion had gone into its making and firing, and love and devotion went into its use. Not just an inanimate object, the bowl is also a womb, heart, bond between generations: through sacred mystery, life somehow . . . appears. An object like this cannot be bought. Manufactured products rarely carry this depth of meaning.

So baking bread got Bruce through, gave him something to do, something real, relevant, nourishing. Baking bread sustained him, and soon it was sustaining others. He'd trade bread for firewood, for home-made beer, for groceries, for car repair. Soon someone was offering him space in a small local store, "Put a few loaves out here, to sell, why don't you? It's damn good bread." And so a business started which he called Bruce Bread Bakery.

Bruce kept feeling his way along. One day, he said, he drove to Santa Rosa, thinking he might expand his business to the big city. Sitting in his car at a stoplight, sweating, breathing exhaust fumes, he decided it just wasn't worth it, and headed back to the fresh air of the country. Two of his daughters joined him in the business, and after five or six years Bruce had begun to wonder if maybe he wasn't ready to go on to something else. "Now what?" he queried me. "Follow the gift," was my response.

I used to stop by on my way to Oz Farm, but I've been out of touch for several years now — love and blessings, Bruce.

Greg Adams, who started The Baker in Milford, New Jersey, is another one of my fans. The *Bread Book* inspired his early efforts to develop a line of breads, and when he needed to get away for a few days in 1979 or 1980, he made a pilgrimage to California, first looking for me at the Tassajara Bakery. Purchasing some Cottage Cheese Dill Bread to try out, he "inhaled a whole loaf." Told that I was a waiter at Greens Restaurant, he came to see me there and introduced himself. He filled out his weekend with a Giants game and a tour of the Napa Valley wine region.

The *Bread Book* really resonated with him, he says, and, "because your book speaks from the heart, it speaks for me too. I associated the stuff I was making with what you were saying." Greg is wonder-fully enthusiastic, becoming inspired by one thing after another, most lately blue-green algae. Once in a while he would send me a care package, which always included some of his superb Bruffles, a thick, fudgy brownie reminiscent of chocolate truffles. Wishing you well, Greg.

And my long-time baker friend, Kerry Smith (from Bloomington) later spent seven years founding and managing Signature Breads in the Boston area. One year when I visited he was opening his third plant and grossing close to a million dollars a month in sales. All his breads were partially baked (or "parbaked") and quick-frozen. The flour was hosed directly into silos, the oil into tanks — *sacks* and *tins*? Are you kidding?

Customers would pick up the breads at the loading dock — I got tired of being in the trucking business, Kerry told me — and then bake them off on their own premises and serve hot out of the oven, or bag under their own label. Kerry is smart, hard-working, and compassionate. He sought out good people and was able to empower them to take responsibility and be accountable. One of his plant managers, Fitzroy, was from Haiti, and his bakeries employed people from fifteen or more countries. His team of people produced a whole range of high-quality breads. I cannot say enough about his commitment to excellence and his genuine good-heartedness. After seven years, Kerry's bakery sold for a handsome profit. Always in my heart, Kerry.

More locally, I love the Bovine Bakery, which opened in Point Reyes Station a few years back. When I first heard the name, I thought it was strange because of the connotations of large, round, and slow, and who wants to think of that when visiting a bakery? Yet this is an area with many dairies and hence something of a fascination for cows, and I have become joyfully accustomed to hearing people say, "Have you been to the Bovine?" or "Meet you at the Bovine." When I sit for more than a few minutes at the counter inside or on the bench outside, I always encounter someone I know, often people I haven't seen for a while. The bakery brings us together. Thank you, Bridget.

I feel fortunate to have found a way to nourish myself and others — and grateful that so many others share my passion for baking. Growing up I often felt lonely, estranged, disconnected. While at Antioch College I once got an "A" on my paper about alienation and anxiety and how to deal with them — and felt just as alienated and anxious! How is this book knowledge going to help, I wondered. Learning to bake bread is one of the things that saved me. Real work that I could do with my hands and my body and not just my head, keeping track of one thing or another. Real work like what plants do so well—taking root and growing.

Studying Zen with Shunryu Suzuki Roshi and being a member of the meditation community at Tassajara was another thing that saved me. Working for the benefit of one's fellow community members feels so meaningful and fulfilling compared to working in someone else's business. One joins the Zen family, which like bread-baking has a lineage of ancestors. Sharing in forms of practice carries on the family tradition. Sitting meditation in the stillness—fortified and made vibrant with one's companions also sitting—deepened my capacity to experience each moment closely and carefully. Kind-hearted attention finds its way to the surface. We offer our good-hearted efforts.

Pivotal in our lives is finding ways to provide for ourselves and our families, ways to benefit our communities. Baking for one another is a piece of this work, which may be physically challenging and emotionally draining at times, but it is also loving what you do, in companionship with flour and water, sugar and butter; loving what you do that nourishes your spirit and others' stomachs, and provides convivial space for family and neighbors to get together.

Thank you for your endeavors to nourish yourself and others. My gratitude and love to all of you who have been baking or will be baking, whether it is large or small, home-based or commercial. Please continue your warm-hearted efforts.

A Body Baking

While we worked together in the garden, a friend told me, "Flowers are angels from distant stars come down to earth with their heavenly message. The more time you spend with them, the more you touch them, tend them, sit with them, regard them, the more you hear their message."

"And what do you listen with?" I asked.

"You listen with your eyes and nose, hands and ears."

"And what about the cheeks and the ankles? Is it not a whole body listening?"

"Yes, a whole body listening."

What to do, how to tend, how to pass on the message: star food, angel food, transfixed body, body of light, food body, cooking body. Body of bread, cake-body, body of biscuits, seed-body: the Heart of Compassion enters the truth of the moment, listening, hearing, responding.

When I cook, another body comes alive. Not the body of walking or typing, not the body of sitting or talking, certainly not the body of driving or TV-watching, but the body of cooking: a body alive to flavors and fragrance, a body ready to touch and be touched, a body which eats with eyes and nose as well as mouth, eats and is eaten. Hands awaken, boundless with their own knowledge, picking up, handling, putting down. A whole body, nothing but food, offering.

This body cooking is also the body of my child, the body of my parents, an interconnected body, focused on feeding. A body holding my daughter, a body being held: taking your tiny hand in mine, your first day of school, we walk slowly knowing life will never be the same again, and this moment is precious. My hand in yours as I breathe one last breath, nothing left to accomplish, no one left to please, I let go and relax. No one tied down, no one to be freed. No more worry about not being perfect.

My everyday body, my everyday world has less clarity and focus, less sparkling presence. And I begin to wonder, "What can I do? How can I help?" What a gift in the midst of all the turmoils of life—life-threatening automobile and bicycle accidents, family illness and death, relationship disjunctions and housing dislocations (not to mention even *bigger* issues)—to find a simple way of expressing warmth and kindness: the offering of bread. My grandmother—see Christmas

Braided Bread   lived long enough (into her nineties) to see her husband and all but one of her children die — and went on baking bread.

Working to bake bread can renew our spirit, and with this work we renew the world, our friends and neighbors. We are reconnecting with the earth, reconnecting with our common heritage, our shared life and livelihood — we have something to eat. Please carry on — the work of feeding, the work of the heart. Bread cannot live by words alone. Thank you for your goodhearted effort that brings it alive. Put some time into it: you and the dough — ripening, maturing, baking, blossoming together.

Edward Espe Brown
Inverness, California
January 2009

The Tassajara Bread Book

Ingredients

Love is not only the most important ingredient:
it is the only ingredient which really matters.

— *from a cookbook by a British chef*

THE INGREDIENTS LISTED ARE MOSTLY *WHOLE* FOODS.
Wholeness means that the flour, meal (a coarser grind than flour), or
flakes contain all the elements of the whole grain, particularly the
germ, that part of the grain kernel from which the grain would sprout
if planted. So this germ is the most life-containing, life-giving part of
the grain. Studies show this in terms of its being higher in vitamins and
essential oils than other parts of the grain.

For this reason whole cornmeal, which contains the germ, will have
a greater life-containing, life-giving quality than the "degermed" cornmeal found in supermarkets. Whole cornmeal is a *live* food — it spoils
when the oil in the germ becomes rancid. Degermed cornmeal is a
dead food, as it lacks the germ (of life). Hence, it can be kept on grocery
shelves for months without spoiling, though like all milled grains it
does become stale.

In any case, best to buy grain products as freshly milled as possible
and to preserve their freshness by refrigerating them in sealed jars or
plastic bags. But don't let a lack of whole grain products keep you from
making bread. Most of the recipes can be made with regular white
flour, if necessary.

Whole wheat flour provides the basic foundation of bread. With a deep, full-flavored, hearty wheat taste, it contains all the elements of the wheat kernel: flour, bran, and germ. The bran and germ have good amounts of B vitamins. Stoneground whole wheat flour has a fresher taste and higher nutritional properties than flour produced from high-speed milling, because of the lower temperatures of stone grinding. Wheat flour contains the highest amount of gluten, a substance that holds air in the dough and expands like hundreds of small balloons, giving dough its elasticity. For this reason most of the bread recipes include at least one-half whole wheat or unbleached white flour.

Unbleached white flour is mechanically refined to remove the bran and germ, has not been chemically treated, and contains no preserving chemicals. Compared with the standard all-purpose bleached white flours, it has a distinctly *live* taste. The high gluten content of white flour makes it particularly useful in breadmaking. Small amounts of this flour (10 percent) give lightness and increased workability to (whole wheat) bread doughs. If bread dough is too heavy or too sticky, add more white flour next time. Use it also for special occasions and particular recipes that are lighter and more delicate.

Rye flour contains less gluten than wheat does and tends to produce a fine-textured, moist, dense bread. Small amounts (10 to 15 percent) add smoothness and workability to doughs with a high proportion of granular ingredients, such as corn-rye, rye-oatmeal. Large amounts of rye flour tend to produce a sticky dough.

Cornmeal gives breads a more crumbly texture, a crunchiness and sweetness. *Whole* cornmeal, though it spoils more readily, is superior in taste and nutriment to the degermed cornmeal found in supermarkets. Meal is a coarser grind than flour.

Millet meal, though somewhat bland-tasting, adds a surprising crunchy richness to breads.

Rolled oats make bread chewy, moist, sweet. Their white flakes often make a beautiful mosaic in molasses-darkened breads. To make rolled oats, as distinct from oatmeal, whole oat kernels are pressed flat between rollers. Oatmeal has most often been subjected to a greater amount of processing. Oats are the grain richest in minerals, salt, fat, and protein.

Barley flour is particularly delicious in breads if pan-toasted before being added to the bread dough. As such it gives breads a sweet, moist, cake-like quality.

Brown rice flour is sweet and will tend to make bread moist, dense, and smooth. Cooked brown rice gives bread a moist, chewy character.

Buckwheat flour has a very distinctive taste and, while tending to make bread heavy, it is full of warmth — a good winter food.

Whole grains and cracked grains should be cooked before being added to bread. When you use cooked grains, less water or more flour will be necessary to make the same quantities.

Yeast is a microscopic fungus that, as a byproduct of its existence, makes bread rise. All yeasted recipes use active dry baker's yeast.

Milk makes bread smoother, softer, and more cakelike, and thus softens the full-bodied flavor of the grain. Recipes call for dry milk, though whole milk can be used if scalded (heated to just below boiling) and then cooled to lukewarm. This has to do with killing various enzymes which would otherwise interfere with the activity of the yeast.

Eggs will make bread lighter, more airy, and tender and will give a golden color.

Oil makes a richer-tasting, cakier bread. Nonhydrogenated liquid vegetable oils are more readily digested and usefully assimilated by the

body than hydrogenated (solidified or hardened) oils such as short-
ening and margarine, though the use of these hardened oils tends to
make a flakier dough. For a while there (I don't know — the sixties and
seventies?) — margarine was considered healthier than butter, but I
think it's pretty well documented now that commercially hardened/
hydrogenated oils (transfats) are the biggest health risk in terms of clog-
ging arteries. (Process the oil to make it solid outside the body, and
funny thing, it does the same thing inside bodies.)

Cold-pressed oils are likely to be higher in essential fatty acids than
regular commercial oils. Even so, most cold-pressed oils are highly refined, so that they are clear, light, and nearly colorless. Oils in their
more raw state are cloudy and tend to smell strongly of the plant of
derivation. Also they are more *oily*.

Once again it is a question of commercial value as opposed to human
welfare. Those oils which are more highly refined and processed will
keep better (often with the use of preservatives) and are "purer," so they
are more practical for shipping, storing, and selling to a public that
generally prefers the cheaper, "sanitized" product.

Sweetenings tend to stimulate the appetite (more, more). Honey or molasses is used in most recipes calling for sweetening, though in some
cases their use is impractical. "Unfiltered, unblended, uncooked" honey
contains more enzymes and minerals than regular commercial honey.
Molasses, particularly blackstrap molasses, contains valuable amounts
of B vitamins and minerals, including iron. Blackstrap does have a distinctive, strong taste. Honey or molasses will make the bread pleasantly
fragrant as well as sweet. Sugar, particularly white sugar, has a noted
lack of nutritive factors aside from calories. This tends to create an over-
abundance of sugar in the body, eventually resulting in lowered blood
sugar or less energy.

Dates or raisins or other dried fruits may also replace some of the
sweetening.

Salt will give its unique benefits. Sea salt or unrefined salt contains numerous trace elements often lacking in the usual diet.

Carob flour is used in some of the recipes. Carob has a naturally sweet taste similar to chocolate. It is very wholesome, well-balanced, readily digestible food containing good amounts of B vitamins, vitamin A, minerals, and protein, as opposed to chocolate, which is not noted as a balanced food, capable of being a dietary staple. Nonetheless, chocolate does provide satisfaction and pleasure unobtainable from carob.

Utensils

CERTAIN ITEMS WILL ASSIST YOU IN MAKING BREAD, though few of them are strictly necessary. *Heavy brown ceramic bread bowls* are available. These hold and distribute heat well, which helps the bread dough rise. Preheating the bowl (with a few minutes of hot water) allows the baby bread dough to feel at home and warmly held. A *stainless steel bread bowl* won't break. Large pots, clean buckets, or a plastic basin can provide a home for your doughs. *Mixing spoons, wood or metal,* a *set of measuring spoons,* a *1-cup* and a *2-cup measure* are useful, along with a *rubber spatula* for cleaning cups and bowls. But, if necessary, you *can* do all the measuring and mixing with your hands. Most of the recipes are approximations anyway to give you *some* idea. Learn to feel for yourself, through experience and experimentation.

A *good-sized bread board* for kneading is something worth taking good care of. Use it only for breads. Don't cut on it, and store it in a clean, dry place. Keep it clean and dry. A wet towel between the board and the table will keep it from slipping while in use. Kneading right on the table is all right, too, if you keep it carefully cleaned. A table approximately at the height at which your hands rest comfortably allows ease in kneading. (This is usually a lower height than for cutting.) Give yourself plenty of clear open space to work in.

Bread pans, sometimes aluminum and rectangular; 5¼ by 9¼ and 4½ by 8½ inches are standard sizes. For small loaves, use pans 3¾ by 7½ inches. Wash them only once a year, and they will develop dark tempering. The bread will bake faster and not stick. Other possibilities include *cookie sheets, metal cups, glass or enamel pans, small ceramic flowerpots;* let their shape be the shape of your breads. An *oven for baking,* although you can always make any bread into English muffins or crackers if you have a griddle or a frying pan and stove or fire.

About Yeast

To WAIT ON YEAST IS TO FEED, KEEP HOUSE, KEEP IT WARM, clean its air, empty its garbage, and cater to its whims. Getting angry at its failings does not help. Providing patient, loving care and food for growth does. Begin by dissolving the active dry baking yeast in lukewarm water 90° to 105° F. At temperatures much higher than 105°, the yeast becomes very frantically active and soon exhausts itself (the yeast is killed between 125° and 130°); at lower temperatures it lives a more dormant existence, until below freezing, it barely respires.

Most bread recipes say, "Dissolve the yeast in ¼ cup lukewarm water. Scald milk. . . ." This method does of course produce excellent results (and I include some of those recipes here); however, it is sufficient and timely to dissolve the yeast in the entire amount of water and then stir in the powdered milk, in which case the milk need not be scalded.

Yeast needs oxygen to breathe and simple sugars to eat. Though some simple sugars are present in flour, because of the action of enzymes on more complex starch molecules, generally some sweetening is added for the yeast to dine on. Treat it to molasses (mild or a little blackstrap); honey (orange blossom, buckwheat, tupelo, or choice fancy); brown or white sugars; or corn syrup. Living yeast turns the oxygen and sugars into carbon dioxide and alcohols. (Brewer's yeast is an even better alcohol producer.) The carbon dioxide becoming trapped in the glutinous network of dough is what makes the bread rise.

Take care that the carbon dioxide and the alcohols do not build up extensively enough that the yeast suffocates and generally expires in its own wastes. Punching down the dough or otherwise working with it releases gaseous by-products of the yeast existence and freshens its air. Bake the bread, and the yeast dies. Slice it, butter it, eat it. Be thankful.

A note: Dry yeast bought in bulk at a natural foods store costs a fraction of what it costs in those little packets at the supermarkets.

Detailed Instructions for Making Tassajara Yeasted Bread

YEASTED BREAD IS MADE PRINCIPALLY WITH WHEAT FLOUR, which is what gives bread its distinctive elastic texture in dough form and its airy quality when baked. Other grains do not have the gluten content of wheat, but they can be incorporated into the bread to give variation in texture, taste, and nutriment. Rye, corn, millet, barley, rice, oats, and buckwheat may be used. Further variation of flavor and texture involves the use of milk, eggs, oil, butter, sugar, honey, or molasses. Once the dough is ready for baking, there are many ways to shape and bake it.

The Tassajara Yeasted Bread recipe leads into all the other yeasted bread and pastry recipes: Rye-Oatmeal Bread, Cornmeal-Millet Bread, English Muffins, Cinnamon Rolls. Make the basic bread once, and you will be ready to tackle any of the recipes. Give it your time and attention.

Here is an outline of the instructions that follow:

   I. Getting Started
      A. Mixing Up the Sponge
      B. Setting the Sponge to Rise
      C. Advantages of the Sponge Method
  II. Seeing It to the Finish
      A. Folding in Oil, Salt, and Dry Ingredients
      B. Kneading the Dough
      C. Rising and Punching the Dough
      D. Shaping the Loaves
      E. Preparing to Bake and Baking
      F. Storing

Getting Started

All measurements are for the basic Tassajara Yeasted Bread recipe, page 34.

> *3 cups lukewarm water (85° to 105°)*
> *1 1/2 tablespoons dry yeast (2 packets)*
> *1/4 cup sweetening (honey, molasses, or brown sugar)*
> *1 cup dry milk (optional)*
> *4 cups whole wheat flour (substitute 1 or more cups*
> *unbleached white flour if desired)*

Measure 3 cups water and put it in a good-sized bowl. "Lukewarm" does not feel warm or cold on your wrist.

Sprinkle the dry baker's yeast over the water and stir to dissolve. For faster rising and lighter bread, use an additional package of yeast (about 3/4 tablespoon).

Add 1/4 cup sweetening. You can rinse the measuring cup out in the water if you wish. Two tablespoons of sweetening would be quite sufficient for the growth of the yeast; amounts larger than 1/4 cup may be added to make more of a breakfast bread.

Add dry milk and stir to dissolve. Complete dissolving is not necessary (Figure 1), as the ingredients will become well mixed when the batter is thicker. The bread will have a grainier taste and a coarser texture if the dry milk is omitted. In this case less flour will be needed.

If eggs are desired (as in some of the variations), beat and add at this stage, adding more flour as needed for proper consistency of the dough. Or the eggs may be added to the completed sponge *after* the flour is in and the batter beaten.

Then add whole wheat flour a cup or so at a time, stirring briskly after each addition (Figure 2). As the mixture thickens, begin *beating* with a spoon, stirring up and down in small circular strokes at the surface of the mixture (Figures 4 and 5). Scrape the sides of the bowl occasionally

(Figure 3). After 4 cups of flour have been added, the mixture will be quite thick, but still beatable — a thick mud.

Now beat about 100 times (Figures 4 and 5) until the batter is very smooth. Do this at the surface of the dough, ducking the spoon under the surface, then bringing it up above the surface, pulling up the batter in a circular motion. The batter will become more elastic as you do this and air will be incorporated into the sponge.

Setting the Dough to Rise

Cover the bowl with a damp towel to keep off drafts (Figure 6). Set in a warmish place (about 85° to 100°). In the summer almost any place might do. Otherwise set it on top of the stove over or near a pilot light, on a shelf above a hot-water heater, in an oven with a pilot light, or in an oven that has been on for several minutes and then turned off. If the bread is rising in a cooler place (70° to 85°), it will rise more slowly. If it is frozen, it will not rise at all but will when it is thawed. Heat above about 125° will kill the yeast, which is what happens when the bread is baked.

Let the dough rise for about 45 minutes.

Advantages of the Sponge Method

The Sponge Method, omitted in most bread recipes, is advantageous in several ways. The yeast gets started easily in the absence of salt, which inhibits its functioning, and in the presence of abundant oxygen. Gluten (or elasticity) is formed when the sponge stretches in rising, which would otherwise be the product of *your* labor in kneading. This added elasticity makes it easier to incorporate the remaining ingredients and to knead the dough. Even a 10- to 15-minute rising at this point will facilitate the remaining steps.

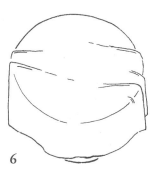

6

7

Seeing It to the Finish

All measurements are for the basic Tassajara Yeasted Bread recipe, page 34.

> *4 teaspoons salt*
> *⅓ cup oil or butter*
> *3 cups whole wheat flour*
> *1 cup additional whole wheat flour (or unbleached*
> *white flour) for kneading*

Folding in is the method used to mix from this point on (Figures 8, 9, 10). *Do not stir.* Do not cut through the dough. Keep it in one piece as much as possible. This will improve the elasticity and strength of the dough.

Sprinkle in the salt and pour on the oil. Stir around the *side* (or bottom) of the bowl (Figure 8) and fold over toward the center (Figures 9 and 10).

Folding in Oil, Salt, and Dry Ingredients

[MAKES 2 LOAVES]

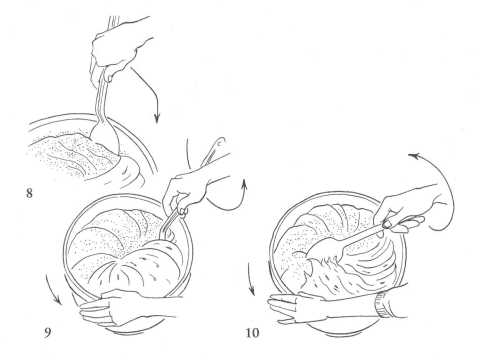

8

9   10

Turn the bowl toward you a quarter turn with your left hand and repeat folding until oil and salt are incorporated (Figures 8, 9, 10).

Sprinkle the dry ingredients on the surface of the dough about a 1/2 cup at a time. Fold the wet mixture from the sides (and bottom) of the bowl on top of the dry ingredients. Turn the bowl a quarter turn between folds (Figures 8, 9, 10). When the dry ingredients are moistened by the dough, add some more dry ingredients. Continue folding. After adding 2 cups of wheat flour, the dough will become very thick and heavy, but don't be intimidated. Continue folding in an additional cup of flour (Figures 11 and 12) until the dough comes away from the sides and bottom of the bowl, sitting up in the bowl in a big lump (Figure 12). The dough is ready for kneading when it can be turned out of the bowl in pretty much of a piece, except for a few remaining scraps (Figure 13). Take time to scrape the bowl (as well as the spoon), and lay the scrapings on top of the dough on a floured board. It is not necessary to wash the bread bowl at this point; just oil it lightly.

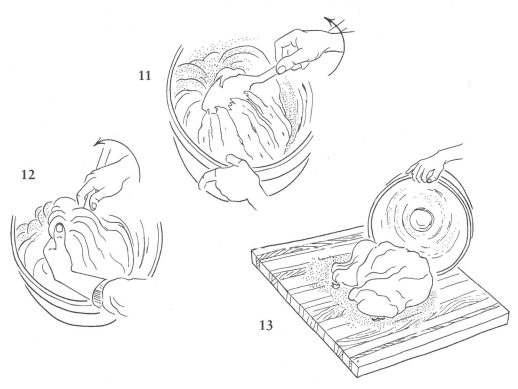

11

12

13

The kneading surface, a board or a tabletop, should be at a height on which your hands rest comfortably when you are standing straight. You need to be able to exert some downward pressure. Keep the surface floured enough to prevent the dough from sticking during kneading. The purpose of kneading is to get the dough well mixed, give it a smooth, even texture, and further develop its elasticity.

Flour your hands and sprinkle some flour on top of the dough.

Picking up the far edge of the dough, fold the dough in half toward you, far side over near side (Figure 14), so that the two edges are approximately lined up evenly (Figure 15).

Place your hands on the near side of the dough so that the top of your palms (just below the fingers) are at the top front of the dough (Figure 15).

Push down and forward, centering the pushing through the heels of the hands more and more as the push continues (Figure 16). Relax your fingers at the end of the push. Rock forward with your whole body

Kneading the Dough

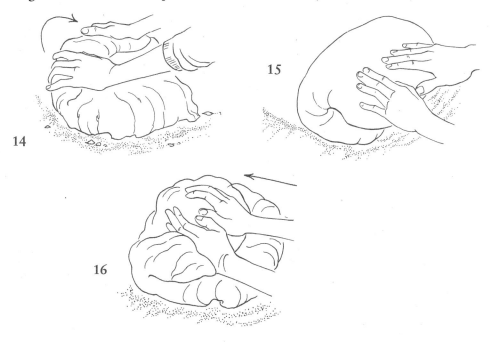

14

15

16

rather than simply pushing with your arms. Apply steady, even pressure, allowing the dough to give way at its own pace. The dough will roll forward with the seam on top, and your hands will end up about two-thirds of the way toward the far side of the dough. Removing your hands, see that the top fold has been joined to the bottom fold where the heels of the hands were pressing (Figure 17).

Turn the dough a quarter turn (Figures 18 and 19); clockwise is usually easier for right-handed persons. Fold in half toward you as before (Figure 19) and rock forward, pushing as before (Figure 16).

Turn, fold, push. Rock forward. Twist and fold as you rock back. Rock forward. Little by little you will develop some rhythm. Push firmly yet gently so that you stretch but do not tear the dough.

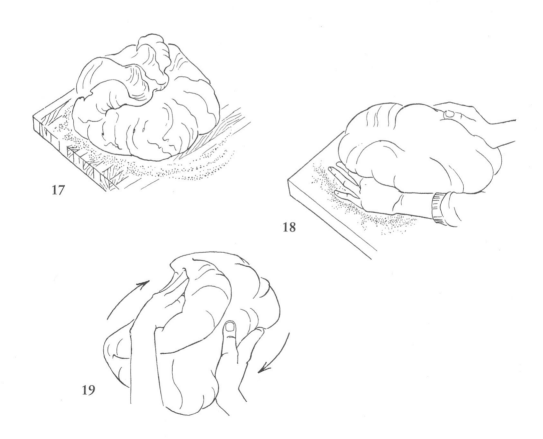

17

18

19

Add flour to the board or sprinkle it on top of the dough as necessary to keep the dough from sticking to the board or your hands. As you knead, the dough will begin stiffening up, holding its shape rather than sagging; it will become more and more elastic, so that it will tend to stretch rather than tear. It will stick to your hands and the board less and less until no flour is necessary to prevent sticking. The surface of the dough will be smooth and somewhat shiny.

As you continue kneading, you may stop occasionally to scrape the bread board (Figure 20) and rub dough off your hands, and incorporate these scraps into the dough. Then reflour the kneading surface.

When you are finished kneading, place the dough (Figure 21) in the oiled bread bowl smooth side down, and then turn it over so the creases are on the bottom (Figure 22). The oiled surface will keep a crust from forming on the top of the dough.

Cover the dough with a damp towel and set it in a warm place.

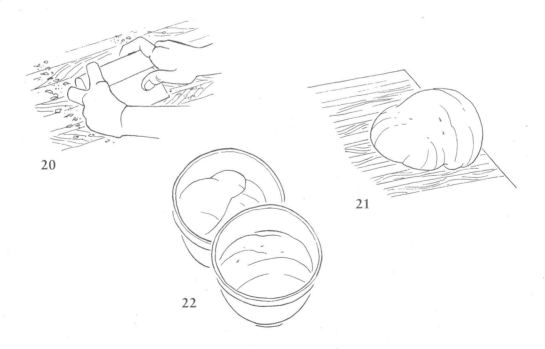

20

21

22

Rising and Punching the Dough

Let the dough rise 50 to 60 minutes, until nearly doubled in size (Figure 23).

"Punch down" by pushing your fist into the dough, as far as it will go, steadily and firmly. Do this maybe fifteen or twenty times all over the dough (Figure 24). It will not punch down as small as it was before rising. Cover.

Let rise 40 to 50 minutes, until nearly doubled in size. If you are short for time, the second rising may be omitted. The loaves will be slightly denser.

Shaping the Loaves

Start the oven preheating. (Adjustment of oven temperatures may be necessary. Electric ovens, especially, should probably be set 25° lower than indicated temperature.) Turn the dough onto the board (Figure 25). If it is of the proper consistency (i.e., moisture content), you won't need much flour on the board. If it is too wet, it will stick on the board. Use flour as necessary. If it is too dry, the folds will not seal together easily. It's too late now, but add less flour next time. (Dipping your fingers in water or oil as you are shaping might provide a bit of "glue.")

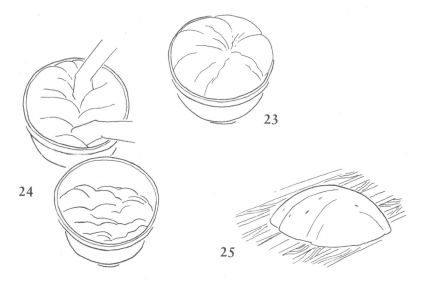

23

24

25

Shape the dough into a ball by folding it to the center all the way around (Figure 26) as in kneading without the pushing (Figure 27). Turn smooth side up, and tuck in the dough all the way around (Figure 28).

Cut into two even pieces (Figure 29). Shape each piece into a ball, and let them sit for 5 minutes.

For each loaf, knead the dough with your right hand (Figure 30). Turn and fold it with your left hand (Figure 31). Do this about five or six times until dough is compact. This gives the loaf added "spring," similar to winding a clock. After the final push, turn the dough a quarter turn.

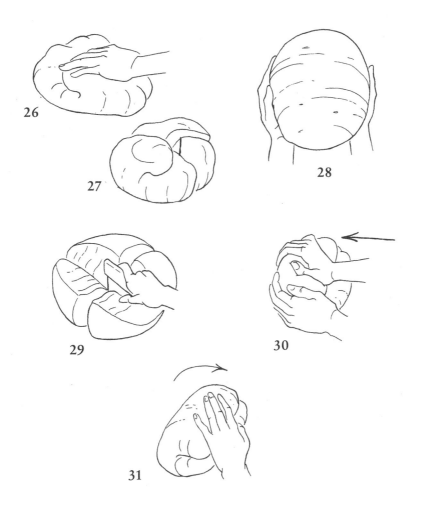

26

27

28

29

30

31

Beginning at the near edge, roll up the dough into a log shape (Figure 32). With the seam on the bottom, flatten out the top with your fingertips (Figure 33). Square off the sides and ends (Figure 34). Turn the dough over and pinch the seams together all the way along it (Figure 35).

Have bread pans in a stack. Put some oil in the top one and turn it over, letting it drain into the next one (Figure 36). Place a loaf in the oiled pan with the seam up. The dough can fill the pan one-half to two-thirds full. A 4 1/2- by 8 1/2-inch pan will make a loaf smaller but higher than a 5 1/4- by 9 1/4-inch pan.

Flatten the dough with the backs of your fingers (Figure 37). Turn the loaf over so that the seam is on the bottom (Figures 38 and 39). Press it again into the shape of the pan with the backs of your fingers (Figure 37).

Cover. Let rise 20 to 25 minutes from the time you finished the last loaf, depending partly on how long you take to make the loaves and partly on how fast the dough is rising. The center of the loaf will be at or close to the top of the pan by this time (Figure 40).

Preparing to Bake and Baking

Cut the top with slits 1/2 inch deep to allow steam to escape (Figure 41). For a golden brown, shiny surface, brush the surface with egg wash: 1 egg beaten with 2 tablespoons water or milk.

Sprinkle with sesame seeds or poppy seeds if you wish.

32

33

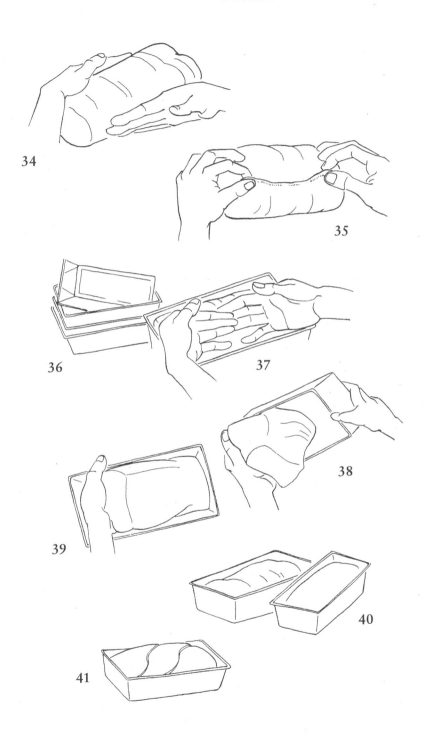

34

35

36

37

38

39

40

41

Bake at 350° for 30 to 60 minutes. (Smaller loaves will bake faster.) When done, the tops should be shiny golden brown, the sides and bottoms should also be golden brown, and the loaf will resound with a hollow thump when tapped with a finger.

Remove from pans to let the loaves cool. For clean-cut slices, let cool one hour or more before cutting.

Storing

When completely cooled, bread may be kept in a sealed plastic bag in the refrigerator. Finished bread may also be frozen and thawed for later use, with slight impairment of flavor and freshness. Somewhat stale bread may be freshened by heating in a 350° oven for 10 to 15 minutes. Dry bread can still be used for toast or French toast, croutons, or bread crumbs.

For zweiback, cut dry bread into cubes and rebake at 200° until crunchy and dry.

Rolls and Other Shapes

Though they are usually made from a dough rich with butter and eggs, rolls can also be made from any bread dough. If short for time before a meal, you may wish to take advantage of the fact that rolls bake more quickly than bread and can be served immediately out of the oven, whereas bread must cool before it can be well sliced.

Expect 12 to 15 rolls per loaf of bread dough.

General Directions for Rolls

Form into a log shape about one loaf's worth of bread dough; the log should be 1½ to 2 inches in diameter (Figure 42) and is formed by rolling the dough between your hands and the bread board.

Section the log into equal-sized pieces (Figure 43).

Shape it into one or more of the following types of rolls or some other shape.

Let rise 20 minutes.

Apply Egg Wash (and sprinkle with poppy or sesame seeds).

Bake about 25 minutes at 375° until nicely browned.

PLAIN ROLLS (THE SIMPLEST AND PLAINEST)
Place the sectioned pieces on edge or flat on a greased sheet or a sheet sprinkled with cornmeal (Figure 44).

CLOVER LEAF ROLLS
Divide sections into three pieces. Shape each into a ball. Place three balls in a greased muffin cup (Figures 45 and 49).

SNAIL OR SPIRAL ROLLS
Roll each section into a length about 6 inches long. Coil it up and place in a greased muffin cup (Figures 46, 47, 49).

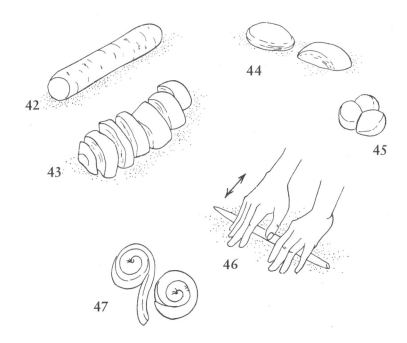

42

44

43

45

46

47

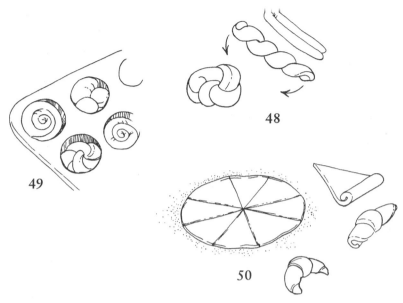

FLOWER ROLLS

Roll each section into a length 8 inches long. Fold double, end to end, and twist. Then coil it and place it in a greased muffin cup (Figures 48 and 49).

BUTTERHORN OR CRESCENT

Rather than shaping the dough into a log at the start, roll it out in a circle about 1/4 inch thick. Brush with melted butter. Cut into 8 to 12 wedges. Roll it up, starting from the wide end. Twist to form a crescent. Place crescent on greased sheet (Figure 50).

Fruit-Filled Loaves (Or Ricotta-Olive Bolso)

Any yeasted bread dough can be made into fruit-filled loaves braided on top. Make any size loaf.

Flatten dough into a rectangle about 1/2 inch thick by rolling, pressing, and/or stretching (Figure 51).

Arrange sliced fruit pieces (apple, banana, peach, plum, pear, apricot, nectarine) down the center third of the dough (Figure 52).

Sprinkle on brown sugar if you like and your choice of spices: cinnamon, allspice, nutmeg, mace, anise.

(Or use the ricotta-olive filling, page 44, for Bolso in place of the fruit.)

Make diagonal cuts in the dough about ½ inch apart from near the fruit out to the edge.

Fold the strips alternately over the fruit, stretching and twisting slightly to form a compact loaf (Figure 52).

Place loaf in a baking pan or on a greased baking sheet.

Let rise 20 minutes.

Apply Egg Wash (and sprinkle with poppy seeds).

Bake at 350° for 45 to 50 minutes or until golden brown.

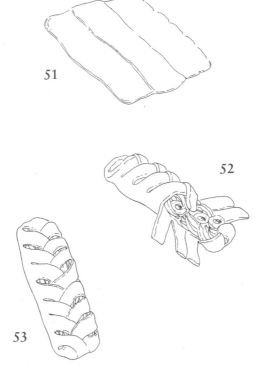

51

52

53

Yeasted Breads

THE FIRST RECIPE IS A BASIC ONE THAT OFFERS AMPLE opportunity for variation and experimentation. This is the yeasted bread that visitors to Tassajara Zen Mountain Center have come to know and enjoy, the bread that hundreds of people take home with them each summer.

Now you can make it yourself and invent your own variations. You can enjoy the aroma of freshly baked bread in your kitchen. Nothing is difficult about this recipe, as there is a wide margin for error, adaptation, and experimentation. If you have never made bread, your first batch is going to be better than nothing. After that, no comparison! Each batch is unique and full of your sincere effort. Offer it forth.

Now that a number of years have passed since this book first came out, I can say that I have heard over and over again from people that they could finally make bread—following the basic recipe and the *Detailed Instructions*—after never having been able to bake before.

Tassajara Yeasted Bread

[MAKES 2 LOAVES]

This is the basic Tassajara yeasted bread recipe, from which all of the others follow. (For a thorough, illustrated explanation of the directions, see *Detailed Instructions for Making Tassajara Yeasted Bread,* page 14.)

I. *3 cups lukewarm water (85° to 105°F)*
   1½ tablespoons dry yeast (2 packets)—for faster rising
       and lighter bread, use an additional packet of yeast
       (about ¾ tablespoon)
   ¼ cup sweetening (honey, molasses, or brown sugar)
   1 cup dry milk (optional)
   4 cups whole wheat flour (substitute 1 or more cups
       unbleached white flour to make the dough a bit
       more cohesive, if desired)

II. *4 teaspoons salt*
   ⅓ cup oil or butter
   3 cups additional whole wheat flour
   1 cup whole wheat flour for kneading

Dissolve the yeast in water.

Stir in sweetening and dry milk.

Stir in the 4 cups of whole wheat flour to form a thick batter.

Beat well with a spoon (100 strokes).

Let rise 45 minutes.

Fold in the salt and oil.

Fold in an additional 3 cups of flour until the dough comes away from the sides of bowl.

Knead on a floured board, using more flour (about 1 cup) as needed to keep the dough from sticking to the board, about 8 to 10 minutes, until the dough is smooth.

Let rise 50 to 60 minutes until doubled in size.

Punch down.

Let rise 40 to 50 minutes until doubled in size.

Shape into loaves and place in pans.

Let rise 20 to 25 minutes.

Brush tops with Egg Wash (page 45).

Bake in a 350° oven for 1 hour, or until golden brown.

Remove from pans and let cool — or eat right away.

VARIATIONS

The recipes in this section, with the exception of the Ricotta-Olive Bolso and two Focaccia breads, are examples of possible variations of the basic Tassajara Yeasted Bread. All quantities are for two loaves. For each recipe, proceed as with the basic recipe. Variations include the following:

- Water is partially replaced with eggs, sour cream, buttermilk, or mashed banana in some of the recipes.
- If you like a lighter bread (and quicker risings), use an additional package of yeast.
- The possible sweetenings each have a particular nature and are in some instances specified.
- The 4 cups of flour that go into the sponge are specified as "2 cups white and 2 cups whole wheat flour" or "4 cups white flour," and so forth, as the case might be.
- For the 3 cups of flour in the second part of the recipe, the following ingredients may be substituted: rye flour, rolled oats, cornmeal, millet meal or whole millet, wheat bran, wheat germ, rice flour, barley flour, soy flour. If cooked grains or cereals are added, additional wheat flour will be necessary to compensate (or the amount of water at the start can be reduced). Generally only one or two of these grains

or flours are added in addition to the wheat flour. When more grains are used, the bread tends to lose the distinctiveness of its taste. The use of rice flour, wheat germ, wheat bran, and soy flour in particular will tend to make the bread heavier and denser, although this is also true of any of the flours besides wheat.

- Use wheat flour as necessary to knead—more (or less) than 1 cup may be required.

Rye-Oatmeal Bread

Darker-colored because of the molasses and rye flour, and flecked with white specks of oats, chewy and moist.

I. *3 cups lukewarm water*
1 1/2 tablespoons dry yeast (2 packets)
1/3 cup molasses
1 cup dry milk
2 cups unbleached white and 2 cups whole wheat flour

II. *4 teaspoons salt*
1/3 cup oil
1 1/2 cups rolled oats
1 1/2 cups rye flour
1 cup (approximately) whole wheat flour for kneading

Proceed with the directions in the Tassajara Yeasted Bread recipe, page 34.

Sesame Bread

This bread has a rich flavor of sesame and a melt-in-the-mouth texture. The sesame meal is so rich with oil that no other oil is needed.

I. *3 cups lukewarm water*
1 1/2 tablespoons dry yeast (2 packets)
1/3 cup honey

1 cup dry milk
2 cups unbleached white and 2 cups whole wheat flour

II. *4 teaspoons salt*
   3 cups sesame meal (more if you can stand it)
   2 to 3 cups whole wheat flour, as necessary to finish
      forming the dough and complete the kneading

Proceed with the directions in the Tassajara Yeasted Bread recipe, page 34.

A good, basic white bread. With the eggs this bread is reminiscent of Challah.

White Egg Bread

I. *2 1/2 cups lukewarm water*
   1 1/2 tablespoons dry yeast (2 packets)
   1/4 cup honey
   1 cup dry milk
   2 eggs, beaten
   4 cups unbleached white flour

II. *4 teaspoons salt*
   1/3 cup butter (or oil)
   3 cups or more unbleached white flour for forming
      the dough
   1 cup (approximately) white flour for kneading

Proceed with the directions in the Tassajara Yeasted Bread recipe, page 34, adding the beaten eggs after stirring in the dry milk. For a Challah-like bread, you could braid it into four or six strands (pages 59–60), brush with Egg Wash, and sprinkle with poppy seeds before the final rise and baking.

Potato
Bread

This white bread is moister and chewier than the White Egg Bread.

I. *2 cups warm water*
   1 1/2 tablespoons dry yeast (2 packets)
   1/4 cup honey
   1 cup dry milk
   3 cups unbleached white flour

II. *4 teaspoons salt*
   1/4 cup oil
   1 1/2 to 2 cups cooked mashed potatoes
   3 cups unbleached white flour
   1 cup or more white flour for kneading

Proceed with the directions in the Tassajara Yeasted Bread recipe, page 34, folding in the mashed potatoes along with the salt and oil.

Summer
Swedish
Rye Bread

Sweet-smelling and scented, a light bread suitable for sandwiches.

I. *3 cups lukewarm water*
   1 1/2 tablespoons dry yeast (2 packets)
   1/3 cup honey
   1 cup dry milk
   Grated peel of 2 oranges
   2 teaspoons anise seeds
   2 teaspoons caraway seeds
   4 cups unbleached white flour

II. *4 teaspoons salt*
   1/4 cup oil
   4 cups rye flour
   1 cup (approximately) whole wheat flour
      for kneading

Proceed with the directions in the Tassajara Yeasted Bread recipe, page 34, stirring in the orange peel, anise seeds, and caraway seeds after the dry milk.

Crunchy, crumbly, and yellow-tinted with the cornmeal and millet, this bread has a warm sunny feeling.

Cornmeal-Millet Bread

I. *3 cups lukewarm water*
  1 1/2 tablespoons dry yeast (2 packets)
  1/4 cup honey
  2 cups unbleached white and 2 cups whole wheat flour

II. *4 teaspoons salt*
  1/4 cup corn oil
  2 1/2 cups cornmeal
  1 1/2 cups millet meal
  1 cup (approximately) whole wheat flour for forming
    the dough and kneading

Proceed with the directions in the Tassajara Yeasted Bread recipe, page 34.

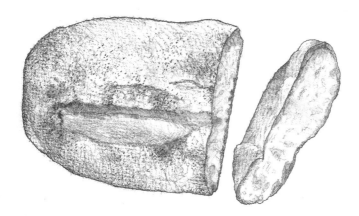

Oatmeal Bread

Moist, chewy, and sweet-tasting.

I. 3 cups lukewarm water
    1 1/2 tablespoons dry yeast (2 packets)
    1/4 cup honey or molasses
    1 cup dry milk
    2 cups unbleached white and 2 cups whole wheat flour

II. 4 teaspoons salt
     1/4 cup oil
     2 to 3 cups rolled oats
     2 to 3 cups whole wheat flour for forming the dough
        and kneading

Proceed with the directions in the Tassajara Yeasted Bread recipe, page 34.

Millet Bread

The millet dots the bread with yellow and provides a flavorful crunchiness.

I. 3 cups whole millet, soaked in 1 1/2 cups very hot water
    1 1/2 cups lukewarm water
    1 1/2 tablespoons dry yeast (2 packets)
    1/4 cup honey
    1 cup dry milk
    2 cups unbleached white and 2 cups whole wheat flour

II. 4 teaspoons salt
     1/4 cup oil
     Soaked millet (see part I above)
     3 cups whole wheat flour
     1 cup (approximately) whole wheat flour
        for kneading

Tassajara Yeasted Bread

SEE PAGE 34

Cornmeal-Millet Bread

SEE PAGE 39

Seed Bread

SEE PAGE 42

French-Style Bread

SEE PAGE 43

Ricotta-Olive Bolso

SEE PAGE 44

Flaky Biscuits

SEE PAGE 93

Rye-Oatmeal Bread

SEE PAGE 36

Start the whole millet soaking in the very hot tap water, and then proceed with the directions for the Tassajara Yeasted Bread recipe, page 34, folding in the soaked millet after the salt and oil in part II.

Fruity, lightly spiced, and especially good for toast and peanut butter sandwiches.

Banana Sandwich Bread

I. *2 1/2 cups lukewarm water*
1 1/2 tablespoons dry yeast (2 packets)
1/4 cup honey
1 cup dry milk
2 bananas, mashed
2 eggs, beaten
2 tablespoons cinnamon
Grated peel of 2 oranges
2 cups unbleached white flour
2 or more cups whole wheat flour for forming
the sponge

II. *4 teaspoons salt*
1/4 cup butter
3 cups whole wheat flour
1 cup (approximately) whole wheat flour
for kneading

Proceed with the directions for the Tassajara Yeasted Bread recipe, page 34, adding the bananas, eggs, cinnamon, and orange peel after the dry milk.

Cinnamon-Raisin Bread

Nothing to it. Makes excellent toast. Proceed with the directions for the Tassajara Yeasted Bread recipe, page 34, folding in 2 tablespoons cinnamon and 1 cup of raisins along with the salt and oil, using some unbleached white flour if you prefer, in place of whole wheat flour.

Nut or Seed Bread

Walnuts? Sunflower seeds? Take your pick. Add a cup or more of any chopped or whole nuts, or seeds of your choosing to the Tassajara Yeasted Bread recipe, page 34. Slightly roasting the seeds or nuts accentuates their fragrant nutty qualities.

Fruit Bread

There are a lot of possibilities besides raisins. Add a cup or more of chopped, soaked, or cooked dried fruit: apricot, prune, peach, date, apple to the Tassajara Yeasted Bread recipe, page 34.

Cheese Bread

Cheese in the bread rather than between the slices makes a flavorful bread for lunch or dinner. It can, of course, also be made into rolls.

I. *3 cups lukewarm water*
1 1/2 tablespoons dry yeast (2 packets)
1/4 cup brown sugar
1 cup dry milk
2 eggs, beaten
2 cups unbleached white and 2 cups whole wheat flour

II. *2 teaspoons salt*
1/2 cup melted butter
3 cups grated cheddar (or other strong-flavored) cheese
3 to 5 cups whole wheat flour as required to form the dough and knead it

Proceed with the directions for the Tassajara Yeasted Bread recipe, page 34, stirring in the beaten eggs after the dry milk, and folding in the grated cheese after the salt and butter.

Crusty, with good wheat flavor. Try a combination of whole wheat and white flour, or use all white flour if you prefer. (The bread has the milk and oil omitted.)

French-Style Bread

I. *3 cups lukewarm water*
    2 1/4 tablespoons dry yeast (3 packets)
    2 tablespoons sugar or honey
    2 cups unbleached white and 2 cups
        whole wheat flour

II. *4 teaspoons salt*
    1 1/2 cups unbleached white and 1 1/2 cups
        whole wheat flour
    Wheat flour for kneading

Proceed with the directions for the Tassajara Yeasted Bread recipe, page 34. With the additional yeast, rising times will probably be somewhat shorter.

To shape the loaves, follow the instructions in the Sourdough section (page 79) or shape into simple rolls. Place the loaves or rolls on a baking sheet that has been sprinkled with cornmeal. Let them rise for about 20 minutes. Brush with water. Bake at 425° for 10 minutes, and then spray or brush the loaves with water. Continue baking at 375° until well browned—another 15 to 20 minutes for rolls, another 35 to 45 minutes for loaves. For added shine and a bit of flavor, brush the tops with garlic butter as soon as the loaves are removed from the oven.

Ricotta-Olive Bolso

[MAKES 12
3- BY 5-INCH
BOLSO]

This is a pocket bread with a filling of garlic-herb cheeses, a hearty, ready-made sandwich. The basic filling recipe is followed by optional ingredients to enliven it further, and, of course, you are welcome to dream up more. Mix up the bread dough first, and while it is rising, make up the filling.

If you need help with the bread instructions see *Detailed Instructions*, page 14.

BREAD FOR BOLSO:

3/4 tablespoon dry yeast (1 package)
1 1/2 cups warm water
1/3 cup dry milk
1 tablespoon honey or sugar
2 teaspoons salt
2 tablespoons butter
3 3/4 cups unbleached white flour or whole wheat
    if preferred

Preheat oven to 350°.

Dissolve yeast in warm water (about body temperature). Stir in the dry milk, sweetening, salt, and butter. Add a couple of cups of the flour and blend thoroughly, beating until the mixture is elastic. Fold in enough of the remaining flour to make a soft dough, then knead several minutes using more flour as necessary. Let rise 45 to 60 minutes.

[MAKES
FILLING FOR
12 BOLSO]

FILLING FOR BOLSO:

1 egg
1 cup grated cheddar cheese
3/4 cup sliced green olives
1 pound ricotta cheese
3/4 teaspoon salt (or to taste)
2 to 3 teaspoons minced fresh oregano or 1/2 teaspoon
    dried oregano

Pepper, freshly ground, to taste
1 or more cloves of garlic

Beat the egg. Mix in the grated cheese and sliced olives. Blend in the ricotta cheese and then season to taste with salt, oregano, black pepper, and garlic.

Use 3 to 4 tablespoons of filling per pocket.

OPTIONAL INGREDIENTS:
Sun-dried tomatoes, slivered
Fire-roasted peppers, slivered
Niçoise olives, pitted and chopped
Other cheeses: feta, provolone, smoked, some
 Parmesan or Asiago

(Keep in mind that some of the optional cheeses are more salty than the cheddar in the basic recipe, so you will want to use less salt.)

To make the bolso, divide the dough into 12 pieces and roll each piece into a rectangle or circle. Mound some filling (3 to 4 tablespoons) on half the dough, then fold over the dough and seal the edges together. Place on a greased baking sheet. Let rise for about 20 minutes, brush the tops with Egg Wash (below), and bake at 350° for about 45 minutes until golden brown. (Alternatively, use the filling to make two filled loaves following the instructions for Fruit-Filled Loaves, page 28.) These are good hot or cold—take them on a picnic!

Beat an egg with 2 tablespoons of cold water or milk. Brush on the top of the bread before baking. More water or milk can be used if you want the egg to cover more loaves.

Egg Wash

*Focaccia –
Olive Oil
Bread with
Sage*

[MAKES
8 ROLLS OR
BABY BREADS]

Here are some wonderful luncheon (or dinner) rolls: crisp-crusted on the outside, bready on the interior. The olive oil and sage provide a change of flavor.

2 cups lukewarm water
1 1/2 tablespoons dry yeast (2 packets)
2 cups whole wheat flour
1 cup unbleached white flour
1/4 cup olive oil
2 teaspoons salt
*2 to 3 teaspoons fresh sage or 1 teaspoon
    dried sage*
2 cups whole wheat flour
1 cup or more unbleached white flour
Olive oil for glazing
Coarse sea salt

Mix water and yeast, and then stir in 2 cups of whole wheat and 1 cup of white flour. Beat well and let rise for 30 minutes.

Fold in the olive oil, salt, and sage, and then fold in the second 2 cups of whole wheat flour and as much white flour as necessary to form a soft dough. Knead the dough until it is elastic and smooth, using white flour as necessary.

Preheat oven to 400°.

Divide the dough into 8 pieces, shape each into a ball, then roll out each ball to a thickness of 1 inch. Leaving the center and edges intact, make four "pie"-cuts (along radii), then place on oiled baked sheets (or parchment paper), and pull the openings apart. Brush with olive oil and sprinkle with coarse sea salt. Let them rise in a warm place about 25 to 30 minutes. Bake at 400° for 20 minutes or until slightly golden.

This is currently my favorite bread, so I love sharing it with people. I walk out the door of my cottage, along the uneven red brick path, out to the front gate where the rosemary bush grows. I prune it so that I can continue to open the gate and walk the pathway. Then I come in, mince the fresh herb, and begin the bread. Often I omit the second rising, so that I can have the bread available somewhat sooner.

I also use this dough to make pizza.

2 cups warm water, under 125°
2 tablespoons dry yeast (about 3 packets)
3 tablespoons fresh rosemary, minced
1/4 cup olive oil
1 teaspoon salt
1 cup unbleached white flour
1 1/2 cups whole wheat flour
3 cups unbleached white flour
Olive oil for glazing
Coarse sea salt

Start with the water, making sure it is not too hot — it should feel just slightly warm on your hand. Stir in the yeast, then the rosemary, olive oil, and salt. Stir in the one cup of white flour and the 1 1/2 cups of whole wheat flour. Beat about 100 strokes. (For more detailed instructions, see page 14.)

Fold in 2 cups of white flour, 1/2 cup at a time. Turn the dough out on a floured board and knead for several minutes using up to one more cup of flour to keep the dough from sticking. Knead until the dough is smooth and elastic.

Let the dough rise for about an hour until it doubles in size. Punch down and let rise another 40 minutes.

To shape into loaves, first divide the dough in half. Shape each half into a ball. (They can be baked in this shape.) I like to flatten out the

Focaccia – Olive Oil Bread with Fresh Rosemary

[TWO MODEST LOAVES; SERVES 4 TO 6 PEOPLE]

ball into a rectangle, then roll it into a log shape. Flatten out the log and make diagonal cuts crosswise, leaving the sides attached. Pull each end lengthwise, so that the loaf forms a "ladder" shape — the cuts are stretched into openings. Place on oiled sheet pan, and brush the top with olive oil. Sprinkle with coarse sea salt. (This is somewhat reminiscent of a soft pretzel.)

Preheat oven to 375°. Let rise about 20 minutes, and then bake about 25 to 30 minutes until browned, top and bottom.

Yeasted Pastries

THE YEASTED PASTRY RECIPES ARE GENERALLY INTENDED for the occasional, special breakfast treat or perhaps for a picnic. Make one on a leisurely Saturday or Sunday morning, or prepare it the night before, bake to a light brown, and then reheat in the morning to finish the baking to golden brown. These recipes require a little more time, a little more effort, and since the result is temptingly delicious, this is perhaps fortunate.

Traditionally this sort of thing is made entirely with white flour, but whole wheat flour, rolled oats, barley flour, and other flours can be supplemented (as in the variations for the basic Tassajara Yeasted Bread, page 34) for added flavor, chewiness, and grainy sweetness.

Also, as you will see, the various doughs are essentially interchangeable in their possible uses for different shapes and fillings.

Yeasted Breakfast Bread Dough

[MAKES 1 LOAF OR 15 TO 18 ROLLS]

This is like the Tassajara Yeasted Bread (page 34), with the addition of eggs and a bit more sweetener and oil. The variations that follow provide ways to make the basic dough into a number of delightful breakfast treats: English Muffins, Swedish Tea Ring, Cinnamon Rolls, Pecan Nut Rolls, Lemon Twist Bread. See what your feeling dictates and your pantry and waistline allow. This particular dough is not so sweet or rich, but is fairly light; more sweetness comes with the fillings. One loaf makes enough to serve 4 to 6 people.

I. *1 cup lukewarm water*
   3 1/2 teaspoons dry yeast (about 1 1/2 packets)
   3 tablespoons honey or sugar
   1/3 cup dry milk
   1 egg
   1 1/2 cups unbleached white or whole wheat flour

II. *3 tablespoons butter or oil*
    1 1/4 teaspoons salt
    1 cup sifted flour: unbleached white or whole wheat
       or your choice
    1/2 to 3/4 cup wheat flour for kneading

The procedure is the same as for Tassajara Yeasted Bread (page 34), except for some different rising times. (You may wish to refer to *Detailed Instructions,* page 14.) Here is a review:

Dissolve yeast in water.

Stir in sweetening and dry milk. Stir in egg. (Thorough mixing at this point is not essential.)

Stir in the 1 1/2 cups of wheat flour until a thick batter forms, and then beat well with a spoon (about 100 strokes).

Let rise 30 minutes.

Fold in butter (or oil) and salt.

Fold in the one cup of flour until the dough comes away from the sides of the bowl.

Knead on a floured board, using more flour (approximately ½ to ¾ cup, depending on what other flours you used) as needed to keep the dough from sticking to the board and your hands. Knead 5 to 10 minutes or until the dough is smooth and does not readily tear.

Let rise 40 minutes.

Now the dough is ready to be made into the Swedish Tea Ring (page 53), Cinnamon Rolls (page 56), Pecan Nut Rolls (page 57), English Muffins (page 58), or Kolaches (page 62). Take your pick.

The dough is rolled up with a fruit filling and then made into a beautiful blossoming flower.

Swedish Tea Ring

FOR THE DOUGH:
Yeasted Breakfast Bread Dough (page 52) or dough
   for Norwegian Coffee Cake (page 61) or Kolaches
   (page 62)

FOR THE FILLING:
1 cup chopped pitted prunes or dates or raisins
½ teaspoon cinnamon (nutmeg or allspice are
   good, too)
1 tablespoon lemon juice or orange juice
¼ cup brown sugar and/or 1 teaspoon
   vanilla extract
⅛ teaspoon salt

Preheat oven to 350°.

While the dough is rising, combine the filling ingredients and simmer until thickened.

After the dough has risen, roll it out on a floured board to 12 by 14 inches. Spread with the fruit mixture (Figure 54). Roll as for cinnamon rolls (Figure 55). Place on a greased sheet and join ends (Figure 56). Cut 1-inch slits with scissors (Figure 57), leaving the inner border of the circle intact. Twist as you wish (Figures 58 and 59). (A straight loaf shape may also be made. Leave the roll straight before slitting with the scissors, and then twist the sections to alternate sides.) Allow the loaf to rise to double in bulk (about 20 to 30 minutes). Brush with Egg Wash (page 45). Bake at 350° for 30 to 40 minutes until golden brown. Be aware that if the loaf is as pictured in Figure 59, the sections in the middle will take longer to bake than those on the outside. Frost with Powdered Sugar Glaze (below) if you wish.

Powdered Sugar Glaze

Here is the simplest way to make a glaze for topping your breakfast pastries. This recipe makes enough for one batch of the accompanying recipes. If you want a lot of glaze, double it.

1 cup sifted powdered sugar
4 to 6 teaspoons milk or cream
or lemon juice

Sift the powdered sugar and mix in the liquid. (Add more liquid if you want to make it thinner.) The glaze may be flavored with vanilla extract or the zested peel of a lemon or an orange.

Frost the pastry when it is hot from the oven.

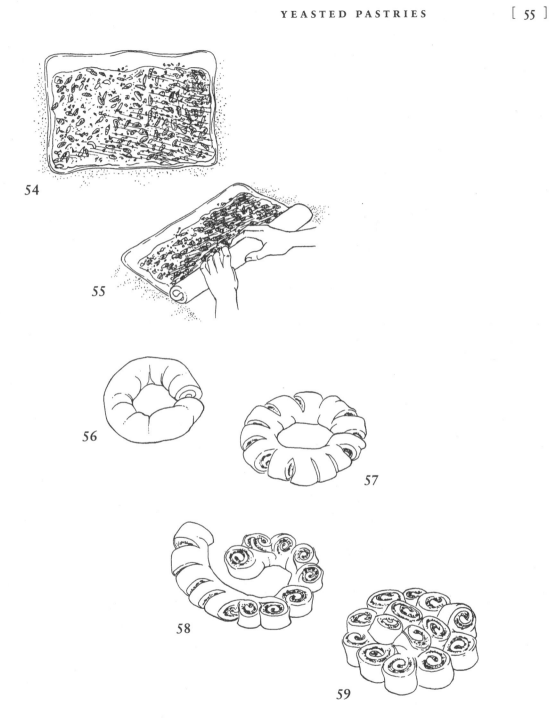

54

55

56

57

58

59

Cinnamon Rolls

What a revelation it was making cinnamon rolls for the first time! They are still one of my favorites. (I also make cinnamon rolls with the dough in Flaky Biscuits, page 93.)

FOR THE DOUGH:
Yeasted Breakfast Bread Dough (page 52) or dough for
  Norwegian Coffee Cake (page 61) or Kolaches
  (page 62)

FOR THE FILLING:
1/4 cup softened or melted butter
3/4 cup brown sugar
1 tablespoon or more cinnamon
1/2 cup or more raisins

Prepare the dough. After it has risen, roll it out on a floured board in a rectangle 1/4 to 3/8 inch thick. Spread on the softened butter or brush on the melted butter.

Sprinkle on the brown sugar, cinnamon, and raisins. (These quantities make a fairly sweet cinnamon roll, but you can use more or less of these ingredients as you prefer.)

Starting at one edge, roll up the dough fairly tight as you would a carpet. (See Figure 55, which shows this same procedure for the Swedish Tea Ring.) Cut the roll in sections about 1/2 to 3/4 inch thick, and place the sections flat on a greased baking sheet, leaving space around them to rise and spread out. Let them rise for 20 minutes.

Brush with Egg Wash (page 45) and bake at 375° for about 20 to 25 minutes, until golden brown.

Frost with Powdered Sugar Glaze (page 54).

Baked on a bed of sugar, butter, and nuts, the Pecan Nut Rolls are turned upside down out of the pan so that they have a sweet, syrupy topping. Since the rolls are nestled in the pan next to each other, they rise up and not out, and make a tender and light roll with little crust.

Pecan Nut Rolls

[SERVES 4 TO 6 PEOPLE]

FOR THE DOUGH:
Yeasted Breakfast Bread Dough (page 52) or dough for
Norwegian Coffee Cake (page 61) or Kolaches
(page 62)

FOR THE FILLING:
¼ cup softened or melted butter
¾ cup or less brown sugar
1 tablespoon or more cinnamon
½ cup or more raisins
1 cup or more chopped pecans (or walnuts
or other nuts)
6 tablespoons butter, in the pan(s)
½ cup brown sugar, in the pan(s)

Prepare the nut rolls according to the directions for Cinnamon Rolls (page 56), adding ½ cup or more of chopped pecans along with the raisins. (You may want to use less sugar in the filling.) Use two cake pans or two pans 8 inches square. Dot the bottom of *each* pan with 3 tablespoons butter and ¼ cup brown sugar, along with an additional ¼ cup or more of chopped pecans. Place the cut rolls next to each other on top of this mixture. Let rise for 20 to 30 minutes and bake at 350° for 30 minutes until golden brown. Turn upside down onto a serving platter.

English Muffins

These favorites can be made with any yeasted bread dough. They keep well, refrigerated or frozen.

Yeasted Breakfast Bread Dough (page 52) or another
yeasted bread dough

Make up a batch of Yeasted Breakfast Bread Dough or make a dough from the Yeasted Bread Recipes, pages 31 to 48 (with or without the addition of eggs). One-third to one-half a batch will make the same number of muffins as the Yeasted Breakfast Bread Dough. (The rest of the batch can still be made into a loaf of bread.)

After the dough has risen, punch it down and let it rest for 10 minutes. Roll out the dough on a floured board about 1/4 to 3/8 inch thick and cut into 3-inch rounds or squares. Sprinkle the tops with cornmeal.

Cover with a dry towel and let muffins rise on the board until doubled in size (30 to 45 minutes).

Bake slowly on an ungreased griddle. For each side start the griddle hot, and then reduce heat to brown slowly, cooking 5 to 8 minutes on each side.

If the middles of the muffins still seem doughy, put them in a 350° oven for a few minutes to finish baking.

Lemon Twist Bread

The tangy lemon scent of this bread freshens the morning air.

Yeasted Breakfast Bread Dough (page 52)
1/2 cup raisins
1 tablespoon grated lemon peel
1 teaspoon freshly grated nutmeg

Follow the Yeasted Breakfast Bread Dough recipe, adding the raisins, lemon peel, and nutmeg to the sponge.

After the dough has risen once, punch it down and let it rise again. Then divide into as many pieces as you would like to braid, roll out each piece into a strand, and braid. (Illustrations for braiding four strands are below; illustrations for braiding six strands are on page 60.)

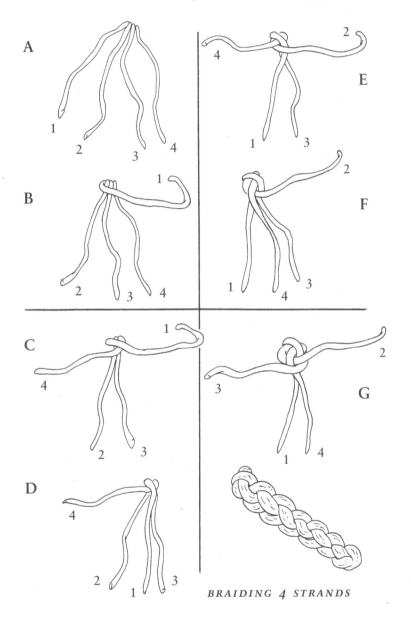

BRAIDING 4 STRANDS

Place the loaf on a greased cookie sheet and let it rise for 20 to 30 min
utes until doubled. Brush with Egg Wash (page 45).

Bake at 350° for 40 minutes or until golden brown. Frost with Powdered
Sugar Glaze (page 54), using lemon juice and grated lemon peel.

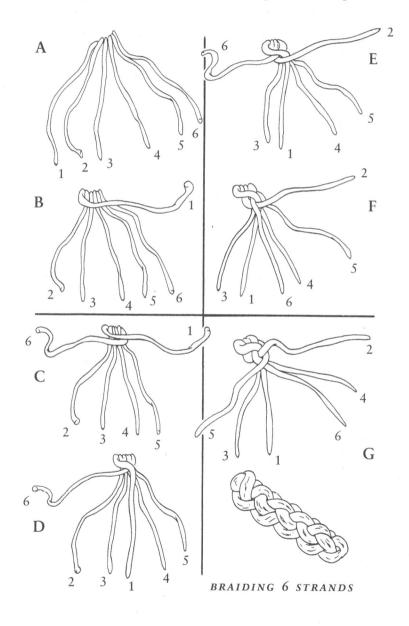

BRAIDING 6 STRANDS

Rich with butter, sugar, and eggs, this dough can be made into a large braided loaf, or used for Cinnamon Rolls, Pecan Nut Rolls, or Kolaches. The recipe makes a larger amount of dough than the Yeasted Breakfast Bread Dough, so you might be prepared to do some of each.

Norwegian Coffee Cake

[SERVES 6 TO 8 PEOPLE]

> *1 1/2 tablespoons dry yeast (2 packets)*
> *1 1/4 cups lukewarm water or milk (if using whole milk, scald and cool to lukewarm)*
> *1 1/2 cups unbleached white flour*
> *5/8 cup brown sugar*
> *1/2 cup butter or oil*
> *3 eggs*
> *1 teaspoon salt*
> *1/2 teaspoon freshly ground cardamom*
> *Lemon or orange peel (optional)*
> *1/2 cup raisins (optional)*
> *3 to 3 1/2 cups white or whole wheat flour, as needed*

Dissolve yeast in liquid and stir in the 1 1/2 cups of white flour, adding a couple of tablespoons of the sugar. Beat well, and set aside to rise.

Cream the butter, and then cream in the sugar.

Beat in the eggs, one at a time.

Fold the butter mixture into the yeast sponge along with the salt and cardamom. Then fold in flour (3 to 3 1/2 cups) as necessary to form a soft dough. Knead the dough until smooth, using more flour as needed.

Let the dough rise until doubled in size (30 to 40 minutes).

Pick a shape (rolls, braided, filled). Place in or on a greased pan. Let loaf rise to double, about 20 to 30 minutes.

Apply Egg Wash (page 45) and bake at 350° to 375° for about 45 to 50 minutes for larger loaves (25 to 30 minutes for small) or until golden brown.

Frost with Powdered Sugar Glaze (page 54).

Kolaches

[MAKES
APPROX-
IMATELY 24
PASTRIES]

Kolaches are little Czech pastries with a sweet filling. Recipes for possible fillings follow the recipe for the dough. These are fun for breakfast, picnics, or parties.

1 1/2 tablespoons dry yeast (2 packets)
1 1/4 cups lukewarm water or milk, scalded and cooled
1 1/2 cups sifted unbleached white flour
1/2 cup brown sugar or honey
3/8 cup butter
2 eggs
1 teaspoon salt
1/4 teaspoon anise extract or 1/2 teaspoon ground anise seed
1/2 teaspoon mace or nutmeg
3 cups (more or less) unbleached white or whole wheat flour

Soften yeast in liquid. Stir in the unbleached white flour and a little of the sugar. Beat well, about 100 times, cover, and set aside to rise.

Cream the butter with the sugar or honey, and then beat in the eggs, one at a time.

Fold the butter mixture into the risen yeast sponge, along with the salt and spices. Fold in additional wheat flour as necessary to form a soft dough. Knead for several minutes, adding more flour as needed to form a soft, smooth dough.

Let rise until doubled in volume. Punch down, divide into individual pieces (walnut to egg size), shape into balls, and place on greased cookie sheets, leaving room to rise and spread. Flatten to 1/2 inch height and let rise for 20 minutes.

Make an indentation in each pastry with your thumb and put the filling in it. Let them rise 10 minutes, brush with Egg Wash or melted butter.

Bake at 350° for 20 minutes, or until golden brown.

Another method to make Kolaches: After the first rising, roll the dough out to a thickness of 1/4 inch, and cut into squares. Place a spoonful of filling in the center of each square, then twist the opposite corners together over the filling. Pinch the corners tightly together or they will come apart. Let them rise for 10 to 15 minutes, apply Egg Wash (page 45), and bake as above.

KOLACHE TOPPINGS AND FILLINGS

POPPY SEED TOPPING
2 cups ground poppy seed
1 cup brown or raw sugar
1/2 cup honey
1 1/2 cups milk
1/2 teaspoon salt

Grind the poppy seeds in a clean coffee mill reserved for grinding spices. Mix well with the remaining ingredients, and cook slowly for 20 minutes until thick yet spreadable. Cool before putting on dough.

BUTTER GLAZE
1 cup brown or raw sugar
1/2 cup unbleached white flour, sifted
1/3 cup butter

Cut butter into sugar and flour, and place on top of poppy seed, prune, or apricot fillings just before placing Kolaches in oven.

PRUNE OR APRICOT FILLING
2 cups cooked, mashed, pitted prunes or dried apricots
1/2 cup honey
1 tablespoon lemon juice

Mix until ingredients are well blended, and see if you want more of the honey or lemon.

Also try cherry, apple, pineapple, peach, or berry filling for Kolaches.

ALMOND PASTE
1/2 pound ground almonds
2 eggs, well beaten
Honey to taste

Grind the almonds in a Cuisinart or in two batches in a clean coffee mill reserved for spices and nuts. Mix with the eggs, and add honey to taste.

DATE ALMOND FILLING
1/4 cup butter
1/4 cup honey
3/4 cup whole pitted dates
1/4 cup almond paste or chopped almonds

Melt butter and sugar together, stir in remaining ingredients, and cook until thickened.

Braided Christmas Bread

[I VERY LARGE LOAF OR SEVERAL SMALLER ONES]

My grandmother must have made this bread every Christmas for sixty or seventy years. Married in 1903, she raised four daughters and a son. She lost her husband and lived long enough to see all her children die except for one daughter — and went on baking bread.

In her room at my Aunt Hattie's in Gregory, South Dakota, the white paint on the ceiling and walls was peeling, revealing the blue underneath, like clouds in the heavens. In a huge vase was a multitude of flowers, fresh and plastic mixed. All around were the fruits of her handiwork: rag rugs made from whatever scraps were available, embroidered tablecloths and dresser runners, crocheted hotplate covers, patchwork quilts.

Although she came to this country at the age of eighteen, even late in life she spoke little English. We spent our time together laughing and giggling — and baking bread. Of course we didn't measure anything, except by hand or eye or feel. Nonetheless here are the numbers.

1/4 cup lukewarm water

2 1/4 tablespoons dry yeast (3 packets)

1/2 cup sugar or honey

2 cups milk, scalded

1/4 cup butter

3 1/2 cups unbleached white flour

3 eggs

1 1/2 tablespoons salt

1/2 teaspoon mace

1 teaspoon vanilla extract

1/2 cup raisins

1/2 cup chopped walnuts or pecans or almonds

1/2 to 1 cup candied fruit peel or citron or cherries (optional)

4 cups wheat flour (with variations as in Tassajara Yeasted Bread)

Dissolve the yeast in the lukewarm water with a little sugar added. Combine the remaining sugar with the milk and butter. When this mixture is cool enough (body temperature), add the yeast mixture.

Add the 3 1/2 cups of white flour to make a soft sponge, stirring well with a wooden spoon. Set aside to rise.

While the dough is rising, separate the eggs, and beat the yolks and whites separately. Fold the yolks into the sponge and then the whites. Let it rise until doubled in bulk, about 40 minutes.

Fold in the salt, mace, vanilla, raisins, nuts, and optional candied fruit. Fold in more wheat flour until a dough is formed, and knead on a floured board, adding more flour as necessary. Knead well (125 to 150 times).

Place in a buttered bowl and let rise until doubled in size—about 50 minutes.

Place the dough on a floured board. Work it into a ball or cylinder and divide into nine equal pieces. Roll each piece into a length of 14 inches. Pinch four lengths together at one end and intertwine them (see illustration showing the braiding of four strands, page 59). Place this on a well-greased cookie sheet to provide the bottom layer of the loaf. Then braid three lengths and place them on top of the bottom layer. Finally twist together two lengths and place them on top of the second layer. Press the braided lengths together well, since they tend to topple over. Straighten before baking, and perhaps while baking.

Now beat up an extra egg, add a little coolish water, and brush the top of the braids all over. Let rise for about 20 minutes, while the oven is preheating to 325°.

Bake for an hour or a little longer until well browned.

Happy Holidays!

Unyeasted Breads

THIS SECTION OFFERS WHAT I CONSIDER TO BE EXCELLENT examples of the sort of breads that can be done without yeast or other rising agents.

Unyeasted breads have a deep, hearty, honest spirit with a certain substantial integrity. Dense and thick-crusted, they require a good bread knife for cutting and a certain endurance for chewing. However, some (such as Overnight Unyeasted Bread) can be made surprisingly light.

No matter how much I mentioned the dense, *bricklike* nature of some of these breads, still I received many letters from people wondering why the bread came out of the oven like a piece of building material. OK, they are not to everyone's taste, but some people really like this sort of thing: "How real," they say, "How flavorful." (If you want something lighter, make a sourdough bread or a yeasted bread.)

Now for some pointers. Warm or boiling water is used because it makes a softer dough that is easier to handle. Make the dough slightly moist before kneading, as more flour can be incorporated during the kneading. Keep enough flour on the board so that the dough does not stick, and scrape up any dough that sticks and reincorporate it into the mass of dough.

Follow the instruction for kneading given on page 19. When the kneading is first begun, the dough will tear rather than stretch, but keep working with it until it is smooth and elastic (about 300 kneads). Resting now and again is permitted.

Make the dough into loaves following the directions given in the *Detailed Instructions* (page 14). When the loaves are in the pans, make a wedge-shaped slit the length of each loaf with a knife. Brush the tops of the loaves with warm water or oil to keep them moist while they sit before baking.

The baking times and temperatures are different for different recipes. You may discover some times and temperatures that you prefer. So much the better.

But remember, if you want a nice, light bread, turn to the Yeasted Breads (or the Sourdough) section.

Tibetan Barley Bread

[MAKES 1 LARGE LOAF]

Many people find this to be one of the best unyeasted breads. But remember, it is dense and thick-crusted. Consider it a relic from the sixties. Does anyone still eat this way?

2 cups barley flour
2 tablespoons sesame oil
4 cups whole wheat flour
1/2 cup millet meal or roasted sunflower or sesame seeds
1 1/2 teaspoons salt
2 tablespoons corn oil
3 1/2 cups boiling water

Pan roast the barley flour in the sesame oil until darkened.

Mix it together with the flour, meal, and salt.

Add the corn oil, rubbing the flour between your hands until it becomes oily.

Add the boiling water a little at a time, mixing with a spoon until a dough begins to form, then mixing with your hands. Keep your hands cool by dipping them in a bowl of cold water. Mix the dough until it has an earlobe consistency, and then knead it until smooth.

Place the dough in an oiled pan. Cut the top lengthwise, making a deep wedge in the loaf. Proof 2 to 6 hours or overnight.

Bake at 450° for 20 minutes on the middle shelf, then 400° on the top shelf. The crust will be tough but the inside tender. You can also try baking at 350° for 1 1/2 hours.

A bread with primitive intensity. It has a deliciously wheaty taste and is remarkably high-rising considering that it has no yeast, unsweetened, with thick crusts and softish interior.

Overnight Unyeasted Bread I

[MAKES I LARGE LOAF]

> *7 cups whole wheat flour*
> *1 tablespoon salt*
> *Warm water as needed, about 3 ½ cups*

Combine the salt with the flour, and add water, mixing with a spoon, until a dough begins to form. Knead 300 times (count them), cover with a wet towel, and let sit 12 to 24 hours in a warm place.

Knead 100 times, shape into a loaf, and place in an oiled pan. Cut the top lengthwise and let proof for 4 hours in a warm place, or 1½ to 2 hours in a 100° to 120° oven.

Bake at 350° for 30 minutes, then at 400° for 45 to 60 minutes. The crust will be dark brown.

If you like this sort of bread, you can of course experiment with the use of other flours in addition to the whole wheat, using a minimum of 4 cups of whole wheat to start with. You could also add ¼ cup of oil per loaf and even a little yeast.

This recipe demonstrates how to make a simple bread using leftover oatmeal and brown rice (though you can also use these in place of some of the water in Tassajara Yeasted Bread, page 34).

Overnight Unyeasted Bread II

[MAKES I LARGE LOAF]

> *3 cups whole wheat flour*
> *3 cups unbleached white flour*
> *1 tablespoon salt*
> *2 to 3 cups leftover cereals (oatmeal and brown rice*
> *   or others)*
> *Warm water as needed*

Mix the flours together with the salt and work in the leftover cereals. If the mixture is too dry to form a dough, add warm water a little at a time until the dough is of kneading consistency. (Since the cooked cereals supply moisture, chances are that not much water will be needed.) On the other hand, if the mixture is too wet after adding the cereals, add more flour to form a dough.

Knead well (300 times), place in a bowl, cover with a wet towel, and let sit 12 to 16 hours in a warm place.

Knead 100 times, shape into a loaf, and place in an oiled pan. Slit the top deeply, and let rise for 2 hours in a briefly heated oven (350° for 5 minutes).

Bake at 375° for 30 minutes, then at 450° for 30 to 45 minutes. The sides of the loaf will be very dark brown.

Unyeasted Dutch Rye Bread

[MAKES 1 LARGE LOAF]

This is the kind of pumpernickel rye with a soft texture reminiscent of salami. Though dense and heavy, the loaf can be thinly-sliced to provide an easy-chewing and flavorful accompaniment to cheeses and cold cuts.

4 cups rye meal (coarsely cracked rye that contains
    some flour)
1 cup cracked wheat
1 1/2 teaspoons salt
2 tablespoons honey or molasses
2 tablespoons oil
1/4 cup wheat bran
3 to 3 1/4 cups boiling water
Wheat germ

Mix all the ingredients together to form a wet dough. Cover and let sit overnight.

Add more bran or wheat flour if necessary in order to shape a loaf. Roll the loaf in bran or wheat germ to coat.

Bake in a covered pan for 4 hours at 200° with a pan of hot water on a lower shelf. (Refill the pan with water as necessary.)

After removing the loaf from the oven, let it cool completely, and then slice; or to keep, wrap it in a moist towel and refrigerate it for one or two days before serving. Slice thinly.

Here is an unusual way to turn leftovers into the "staff of life." Once a "most popular" bread at Tassajara—we still make it on rare occasions—it has a texture similar to sourdough: coarse, but fairly light with a thick crust. (And the sour elements in the leftovers will give the bread extra rise.)

Gruel Bread

> *4 cups rice gruel (cooked-together leftover rice or other*
> *grains, soups, vegetables)*
> *1 teaspoon salt or soy sauce*
> *1/4 cup oil (optional)*
> *6 cups whole wheat flour (amount will vary according*
> *to how moist the gruel is)*

Mix the salt and oil into the gruel (if there are large chunks of broccoli or another vegetable, cut these into smaller pieces), and add flour 1/2 cup or so at a time. Mix by stirring and then by hand until a dough forms with earlobe consistency, firm yet pliable. Knead on a floured board until smooth, about 300 times.

Make into a loaf and place in an oiled bread pan. Brush the top with water and make a 1/2-inch-deep cut down the center of the loaf. Cover with a damp towel, and set in a warm place overnight.

Bake at 350° to 375° for 75 to 90 minutes, until the sides and bottom are dark brown.

Sourdough Breads
and Pancakes

It is surely a wonder of nature that something sour or *spoiled* can make bread rise and delicious besides. Sourdough is probably the easiest bread to make (once you have a good starter), and its flavor is exquisitely distinctive and exciting. I have included in this section Sourdough French, Sourdough Rye, and Sourdough Pancakes.

Making and Using a Sourdough Starter

A *starter* is required in the making of sourdough bread. Growing in the starter are microorganisms that cause the bread to rise and give it its characteristic sour taste. The starter is mixed with flour and water to form a *sponge* (similar to the *sponge* for yeasted bread), which then sits overnight. By morning the entire mixture is sour. Some of the sponge is removed to replenish the starter before other ingredients are added. To replenish the starter, fill a jar or crock (not metal) only half full, as the starter will rise some as it sits. Cover and keep refrigerated.

A sourdough starter can be made by combining 1 tablespoon of dry yeast, 2½ cups warm water, 2 teaspoons sugar or honey, and 2½ cups flour. Cover and let it ferment for five days, stirring daily. The starter may be kept indefinitely in the refrigerator, although it is probably best to use it once a week or so. If liquid rises to the top during storage, stir it in again. The starter and the sponge are both the consistency of thick mud.

Another way to make a sourdough starter is to take any sour food, such as two-day-old or older rice, cereal, coconut, fruit, vegetables, or milk, and mix it with 2½ cups whole wheat flour and enough water to make the dough spongy. Cover and let it sit for 3 to 4 days, stirring daily, until a distinctly sour smell arises. Each starter will be somewhat different in its flavor and efficacy at making the dough rise.

Sourdough Bread

[MAKES 2 LOAVES]

Here is a basic recipe for sourdough bread. The dough can also be made into English Muffins (page 58).

AT NIGHT:
5 cups whole wheat flour
1 to 1 1/2 cups starter (see page 77)
4 cups lukewarm water

IN THE MORNING:
Replenish the starter.
1/2 cup oil
1 tablespoon salt
5 to 6 cups or more whole wheat flour

At night, add the starter to 5 cups of flour without mixing. Then mix together while adding water gradually, until a thick, pasty batter is formed. Beat well. Cover and set aside overnight.

In the morning, remove 1 to 1 1/2 cups from the sponge to replenish the starter, and refrigerate it for the next batch. Now fold into the sponge the oil, salt, and remaining flour gradually with a spoon. When the dough comes away from the sides of the bowl, remove to a floured bread board. Knead for 5 minutes, adding more flour as necessary. The dough will be a little softer and stickier than normal yeasted bread.

Cut into two pieces and form into loaves. To make French Loaves, see page 79. The loaves can also be shaped into balls (and baked on a sheet) or standard loaves (and baked in oiled bread pans). Slit the tops with lengthwise gashes. Allow 2 hours for rising.

Brush or spritz the tops with water and place in a preheated 425° oven for 20 minutes. Brush or spritz the tops with water again, turn the oven down to 375°, and continue baking for an hour or so until the loaves are nicely browned.

A simple variation on the basic sourdough bread provides the hearty, earthy flavor of rye.

Substitute 3 to 4 cups of rye flour for the whole wheat flour in the morning addition. Shape into round loaves and bake on a greased sheet or on a baking sheet sprinkled with cornmeal. Bake as in the basic recipe (page 78).

Sourdough Rye Bread

Here is one procedure for shaping French Loaves. Using unbleached white flour in place of some or all of the whole wheat in the Sourdough Bread recipe will produce a more traditional loaf.

To shape the French Loaves, roll the dough out in a rectangle about 1/4 inch thick on a floured board. Then roll up the dough tightly, as you would roll up a carpet.

Pinch the seam together and roll the loaf about to shape it evenly. Place the finished loaf, seam down, on a baking sheet that has been sprinkled with cornmeal. Brush the loaves with water. Make a 1/2-inch-deep lengthwise slit in the top.

Let rise and bake as for the regular Sourdough Bread loaves (page 78).

Sourdough French Loaves

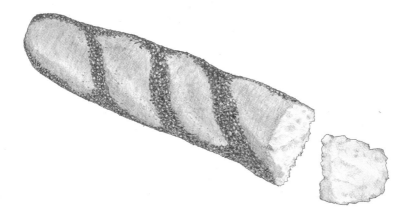

Country French Bread

[MAKES 2 MODERATE LOAVES]

This is about as bread as you can get: flour, salt, water, yeast, and sourdough starter. A wonderfully coarse and bready texture with intense wheat flavor, this bread is basically a sourdough, but with a little yeast boost—one of our perennial favorites.

AT NIGHT:
1 1/2 cups sourdough starter
5 cups whole wheat flour
3 1/2 cups warm water

IN THE MORNING:
Replenish the starter.
1 teaspoon dry yeast
1/4 cup water
1 tablespoon salt
4 to 6 cups unbleached white flour

At night, add the starter to the flour, then mix in the water a little at a time until it is all added. Beat well. Cover and set aside overnight. A warm but not hot place is preferable but not essential.

In the morning, replenish the starter and refrigerate it for the next batch of sourdough bread. Dissolve the yeast in the water and let it sit for 5 minutes. Then stir it into the sponge along with the salt. Fold in the white flour a cup at a time until a dough forms. Remove from the bowl to a floured board and knead thoroughly, adding more flour as necessary.

Divide the dough into two pieces, shape each piece into a ball, and place on an oiled baking sheet. Let the loaves rise until about doubled in size (1 1/2 to 2 hours).

Make a few slits in the tops, brush or spritz them with water, and place the loaves in a 425° oven for 20 minutes. Brush the tops with water again, turn the oven down to 375°, and continue baking for 50 to 60 minutes or until well browned.

Without any milk or sweetening, this bread has an intense pure wheat flavor. So I enjoy making this recipe when I am ready for some *bread*.

Letting the dough sit overnight is vitally important for allowing the flavor of the wheat to "blossom" and this lengthy rising gives the bread a flavor and quality reminiscent of sourdough, but you needn't get involved with starters. For people like me, who are unfortunately not as devoted to baking as we used to be, this bread is earthy, hearty, coarse, and fulfilling.

AT NIGHT:
3 cups warm water
1/4 teaspoon dry yeast
3 cups whole wheat flour

IN THE MORNING:
1/2 cup warm water
1 1/2 tablespoons dry yeast (2 packets)
2 teaspoons salt
2 1/2 to 3 cups whole wheat flour

In the afternoon or evening, stir the yeast and flour into the water and beat (short strokes in and out of the batter) about 100 strokes. Cover and set aside until morning.

In the morning: make sure the 1/2 cup of warm water is cool enough that it will not harm the yeast—about body temperature. Stir in the yeast and let it dissolve, then mix this into the batter from last night. Stir in the salt as well.

Fold in about 2 1/2 cups of whole wheat flour, 1/2 cup at a time. Turn out onto a floured board and knead, using another 1/2 cup or more of flour to keep the bread from sticking. Knead 150 to 300 times. The dough will be smooth and pliable.

Set aside in an oiled bowl and let rise for 3 to 4 hours. Shape into loaves. I like to make log shapes with diagonal cuts on the surface—or you

Overnight Wheat Bread (Wheat Veneration)

[MAKES 2 LOAVES]

could bake it in loaf pans if you prefer. Place on oiled sheet pan and brush with water. Let rise about an hour.

Preheat oven to 375°. Brush the surface once more with water and bake for 45 to 60 minutes, until the loaves are browned, top and bottom.

Sourdough-Raisin Rolls

[MAKES 12 LARGE OR MORE SMALLER ROLLS]

These rolls made by our bakery are unique and unusual—a sourdough sweetened with raisins and cinnamon. Although the rolls are simple to make, some prior preparation is necessary. We keep a sourdough starter just for the raisin rolls, and in addition to this starter a batch of fermented raisins is needed. The raisins take several days to ferment, and the rolls themselves take nearly a day, so plan ahead!

1 teaspoon salt
1 teaspoon cinnamon
4 cups whole wheat flour
1 cup sourdough raisin roll starter (could be your usual sourdough starter for the first batch of rolls)
1 3/4 cups raisin water, see below
1/2 cup fermented raisins, see below
2/3 cup raisins
Whole wheat flour as needed

Note: The sourdough raisin roll starter ends up containing raisins, fermented raisins, and raisin water, unlike the plain sourdough starter. But of course a plain starter can be used for the first batch of raisin rolls.

Mix the salt and cinnamon with the flour. Put the starter on top of the flour, and stir in the raisin water (see below) a little at a time to form a soft dough. When the mixture is too thick to stir, work with your hands. Knead for several minutes and then knead in the fermented raisins (see below) and the dry raisins. Keep the dough on the moist side as much as possible, but add more flour as needed to keep it from being too sticky to work with. Let the dough sit for 20 minutes or so, and then replenish the starter.

Divide the dough into twelve pieces for large rolls or more pieces for smaller rolls. Shape into balls and place them on an oiled baking sheet. Cover with a damp towel and let them sit overnight (15 hours or more).

Bake at 375° for 20 to 25 minutes or until well browned. (Smaller rolls will bake more quickly.)

Fermented Raisins and Raisin Water: Place ½ cup of raisins in 2 cups of water. Cover and let sit for 3 to 4 days, unrefrigerated. Stir daily. If you are making sourdough raisin rolls regularly, you can keep a continuous batch of raisins going. We use all the water and a portion of the raisins each day, and then replenish both.

Sourdough Pancakes

[SERVES 2 TO 6 PEOPLE]

Heavenly.

AT NIGHT:
Mix up sourdough sponge as for Sourdough Bread
    (2½ cups whole wheat to 2 cups water with
    ½ cup starter).

IN THE MORNING:
Replenish your starter store from this new batch.
    For every 2½ cups of whole wheat flour used in
    original sponge, add:
1 egg, beaten
2 tablespoons corn oil
¾ to 1 cup milk
1 teaspoon salt
1 teaspoon baking soda
2 tablespoons brown sugar

After replenishing the starter, mix the sponge thoroughly with egg, oil, and milk. Combine salt, soda, and brown sugar, and sprinkle over batter. Fold in gently. Let sit a few minutes before frying. Smaller sourdough pancakes seem to cook better than larger ones.

VARIATIONS

- Add fresh chopped fruit to batter: apples, bananas, peaches, plums, nectarines, apricots.
- Add chopped nuts or seeds to batter: sunflower, pine, chopped walnuts, chopped almond, toasted sesame seeds.
- Add spices as desired: cinnamon, nutmeg, mace, or coriander.

Pancakes and Other Things to Eat for Breakfast, Lunch, or Dinner

PANCAKES WARM THE HEART WHILE FORTIFYING THE stomach, especially for Zen students who have been breakfasting on cereal, beans, and fruit or pickled vegetables. Oftentimes a first stop on the way out of Tassajara is for pancakes with plenty of syrup. More impatient students, sleepless with desire, have been known to sneak into the still-of-night kitchen and fry up a few of their favorites (with all sorts of optional ingredients in the batter or on top of the finished pancake: honey, tahini, peanut butter, blueberries, bananas, roasted nuts or seeds). Generous souls when satiated, they usually tidy up after themselves and leave a couple of pancakes for the kitchen crew.

No special tricks are involved in making pancakes. Heat a frying pan or griddle until sprinkled-on water dances around briefly before evaporating. Fry the pancakes on the first side until small bubbles appear in the uncooked surface. Turn (once only) and fry the other side. If the center is not cooking or if browning is spotty or uneven, the pan is too hot.

The other recipes in this section — Popovers, Cream Scones, Biscuits, and Bagels — also can make a heartwarming offering any time of the day or night. Coffee cake? As you like it.

Whole Wheat Pancakes

To have originally called these pancakes "entirely exceptional" sounds extravagant after all these years, but they certainly are good, especially served with jam-marbled sour cream or butter and maple syrup. I once received a letter from someone who had eaten these at a café in New Delhi — and aside from Tassajara Bread, these pancakes receive more compliments than any other recipe.

2 cups whole wheat pastry flour
3 teaspoons baking powder
1 teaspoon salt
1 tablespoon brown sugar or honey
2 cups milk
1/2 cup oil or melted butter
3 egg yolks, beaten
3 egg whites, stiffly beaten

Sift the flour with the baking powder, salt, and sugar. If using honey, add it to the milk and oil. Beat the milk and oil into the beaten yolks.

Combine the milk mixture with the dry ingredients until just blended, and then fold in the stiffly beaten egg whites.

Cook on a greased griddle or frying pan. May be made any size — the larger ones will take longer to cook through.

VARIATIONS

- May be made with fruit puree (apple, apricot, peach, pear) in place of the milk.
- Fruit chunks may be folded into the batter. Blueberries, bananas, and apple are particularly good.
- Nut butters may be added to the wet ingredients.
- Roasted nuts or sesame or sunflower seeds may be folded into the batter.
- Cornmeal, rolled oats, barley flour, or buckwheat flour (1/2 cup) may be substituted in place of an equivalent amount of whole wheat flour.
- For waffles, use only 1 1/4 cups of milk.

These are fragrant, but you may still prefer your orange juice on the side.

Orange-Whole Wheat Hotcakes

[SERVES 2 TO 6 PEOPLE]

> 2 eggs, beaten
> 1/4 cup oil
> 2 cups sifted whole wheat flour
> 1/2 teaspoon baking soda
> 1/2 teaspoon salt
> 2 cups freshly squeezed orange juice

Mix eggs and oil, and beat. Combine dry ingredients and add to the egg mixture alternately with the orange juice.

Blend well. Griddle.

O-Konomi-Yaki

[SERVES 5 OR 6 PEOPLE]

Japanese pancakes made with vegetables (and meat) can be served as a midnight meal with warm results. Americans put butter on everything (or used to); Japanese prefer soy sauce, but syrup, no.

1/4 Chinese, green, or red cabbage

1 carrot

1/2 onion

2 celery stalks

1/2 cup meat or fish pieces (optional)

2 cups (or more) whole wheat or unbleached white flour, or both

1 egg, beaten

2 tablespoons brown sugar

1 teaspoon salt

1 tall can evaporated milk or 1 1/2 cups milk

Enough water to make batter

Chop, shred, dice, or thinly slice vegetables (and meat). It is essential that the pieces be small so that the pancakes are not too thick. Mix together the remaining ingredients to form a batter. Fold in the vegetables and proceed to grill. If the pancakes are not cooking in the middle, thin the batter some and cook more slowly. These may also be eaten cold on a picnic.

Cottage Cheese Pancakes

[MAKES 24 SMALL TO MEDIUM PANCAKES]

Creamy and blintz-rich without a filling. Well-received over the years.

6 eggs

6 tablespoons whole wheat or unbleached white flour

1/4 teaspoon salt

2 cups cottage cheese

Separate the eggs, beat the whites stiff, and set aside. Beat the yolks and then beat in the flour, salt, and cottage cheese. Fold in the egg whites. Grill, or fry in buttered pan. Smaller is probably better.

Puffy and eggy buns with space for stuffing.

1 cup unbleached white flour
1/2 teaspoon salt
3 eggs, beaten
1 cup milk
2 tablespoons melted butter

Preheat oven to 450°.

Use a popover pan or regular muffin tins. Mix ingredients thoroughly. Grease the muffin tins and heat in the oven for 5 to 10 minutes. When hot, fill each cup one-third full with popover batter. Bake at 450° for 20 minutes, then reduce the heat to 350° and bake another 10 to 20 minutes. Do not open the oven until after 30 minutes of baking or the Popovers may fall.

Serve with butter, jam, or cheese. Or serve for dinner stuffed with meat or vegetables in cream or cheese sauce; with grains, vegetables, or stuffing; or with a mushroom filling. Heck, or just plain buttered.

Popovers

[MAKES 12 POPOVERS]

Here is a giant, clove-scented popover with apples that makes a quick but memorable breakfast dish.

2 tablespoons butter
Juice of 1 lemon
1 medium apple, sliced into wedges
2 tablespoons brown sugar
1/2 cup flour
1/2 cup milk
3 eggs
Ground cloves

Preheat oven to 400°.

Apple Pancake Sam

[SERVES 2 PEOPLE]

Put the butter into an 8- or 9-inch round baking dish and heat in the oven at 400° for 10 minutes. Do not let the butter brown.

Meanwhile, squeeze the lemon juice over the apple slices and toss with the brown sugar.

In a mixing bowl, combine the flour, milk, and eggs. Whisk briefly until barely together. Batter will be lumpy. Remove the baking dish from the oven and pour in the batter. Arrange the apples in a circle around the dish, putting 2 or 3 in the center. Top with the remaining lemon juice–brown sugar mixture.

Bake for 25 minutes until firm and puffy. Dust with a sprinkling of ground cloves and serve with warmed pure maple syrup.

In the summer use fresh blueberries in place of the apples.

To serve 4, this recipe may be doubled and baked in a 15- to 16-inch dish.

Cream Scones

[SERVES 4 TO 6 PEOPLE]

A guest-season favorite, these scones have a soft, velvety texture and a tangy taste.

1 cup buttermilk, sour milk, or milk
6 tablespoons sugar or honey
1 egg
3 1/2 cups unbleached white (or 1/2 white and
  1/2 whole wheat)
2 heaping teaspoons cream of tartar
1 heaping teaspoon baking soda
1/2 cup melted butter or oil

Note: Raw milk will sour much better than pasteurized.

Blend together the buttermilk, sugar, and egg. Sift in the flour with the cream of tartar and soda. Beat well and gradually add the melted butter. Keep the dough moist.

Add up to ½ cup more flour as necessary to roll out. Roll out ¼- to ³/₈-inch thick, cut into triangular wedges, and dust with flour. Bake slowly on a griddle or in a frying pan over medium low heat so that the center will bake (5 to 7 minutes a side). These can also be rolled out thicker and baked in the oven.

VARIATION
Add ¼ to ½ cup currants or raisins.

Tender, flaky, grandly high-rising, this recipe is adaptable to a number of variations listed below and also can be used as a quick dough for cinnamon rolls.

> *1 cup unbleached white flour*
> *1 cup whole wheat flour*
> *3 teaspoons baking powder*
> *½ teaspoon salt*
> *½ cup butter*
> *2 large eggs (see note below)*
> *½ cup milk*

Preheat oven to 450°.

A note about the size of eggs: the larger the eggs, the more the liquid. So with 2 extra-large eggs, use ⅓ cup milk; use just 1 jumbo egg with the ½ cup milk.

Combine flours, baking powder, and salt. Cut butter into dry ingredients with a pastry cutter or two knives, or rub gently between hands until pea-sized pieces are formed. Make a well in the center and add the eggs and milk. Beat the eggs and milk with a fork until smoothish, then continue stirring with the fork, gradually incorporating flour, until all is moistened. On a floured board, knead the dough just enough to bring it together.

Flaky Biscuits

[MAKES 12 TO 16 BISCUITS]

Roll the dough into a rectangle ½ inch thick. Fold in thirds. Turn the dough a quarter turn, and repeat rolling and folding. Repeat once more. (The rolling and folding make a flakier biscuit.)

To make the biscuits, roll out the dough again to a ½-inch thickness. Cut into rounds with a floured cutter or glass. Place on an ungreased sheet, and bake at 450° for 8 to 10 minutes until the bottoms are browned lightly and the tops slightly golden. Keep an eye on them — they get dry if overbaked.

VARIATION
For sesame seed or sunflower seed biscuits, add ½ cup roasted sesame or sunflower seeds with the dry ingredients.

Basil and Parmesan Cheese Flaky Biscuits

[MAKES 12 TO 16 BISCUITS]

A flavorful biscuit variation well suited to lunch or dinner.

Ingredients for Flaky Biscuits
  (see page 93)
1 ¾ cups grated Parmesan cheese
2 tablespoons minced fresh basil leaves

Follow the directions for Flaky Biscuits, stirring the grated cheese and minced basil leaves into the flour-butter mixture before adding the eggs and milk. Follow the same procedure for shaping and baking the biscuits.

Other cheeses (cheddar, provolone, smoked) and herbs (rosemary, oregano, sage, thyme) may also be used.

A sugary, unyeasted coffee cake with a smooth texture, beautifully laced with cinnamon-nut topping.

Walnut Coffee Cake

[**MAKES 1 LARGE COFFEE CAKE OR 12 SERVINGS**]

1/2 cup butter

1 cup sugar

2 eggs

2 1/2 cups cake flour

1 teaspoon baking soda

1 1/2 teaspoons baking powder

1/4 teaspoon salt

1 1/2 cups sour cream with 1 teaspoon vanilla extract
*   stirred in*

STREUSEL TOPPING:

1 cup chopped walnuts

1/2 cup brown sugar

2 to 3 teaspoons cinnamon

1 1/2 tablespoons cocoa

SUPERSTREUSEL:

1 cup chopped walnuts

3/4 cup brown sugar

2 tablespoons butter

2 tablespoons cocoa

Preheat oven to 350°.

To make the streusel: Combine the list of ingredients and work with your fingers until the mixture resembles coarse meal.

To make the coffee cake: Cream together the butter and sugar. Add the eggs one at a time and beat well after each addition. In a separate bowl, sift the flour together with the soda, baking powder, and salt. Add this to the creamed mixture alternately with the sour cream, making about three additions and stirring well after each one.

Spread half of the batter into a large buttered tube pan or 8-inch square pan and sprinkle with half of the streusel. Spread the rest of the batter on next, and finish with the rest of the streusel. Bake the coffeecake for approximately 45 minutes at 350° or until a toothpick comes out clean. Let it cool in the pan, or remove the sides and serve warm.

Butter Kuchen

[SERVES 4 TO 6 PEOPLE]

A yeasted coffee cake not requiring any kneading: tender, moist, appealing.

1/4 cup lukewarm water
1 tablespoon dry yeast (about 1 1/2 packets)
1/3 cup brown sugar
1 cup milk
1 teaspoon salt
1/4 cup butter
2 eggs
3 1/4 cups unbleached white or whole wheat flour

FOR THE TOPPING:
1/2 cup butter
1/2 cup brown sugar
1 cup unbleached white or whole wheat flour
1 tablespoon cinnamon

Combine the water with the dry yeast and 1 tablespoon of the sugar, and set aside.

Scald the milk, remove from the heat, and pour into a bowl. Add the rest of the sugar along with the salt and butter. Once the mixture has cooled to body temperature, stir in the dissolved yeast.

Beat the eggs with 1/2 cup of the flour. Then add the remainder of the flour to the eggs alternately with the milk-yeast mixture, stirring well after each addition.

Pour batter into a 9- by 13-inch greased pan (or a greased tube pan) and let rise for 45 minutes.

Sprinkle on the butter topping, made by cutting together the topping ingredients.

Bake at 375° for 30 minutes, or until the edges pull away from the sides of the pan and the middle is dry when tested with a toothpick.

Bagels are a lot of work, but fun to make. This dough can also be made into braided bread, or Challah. If you have questions about making a yeasted dough, see *Detailed Instructions*, page 14.

Egg Bagels

[MAKES 12 BAGELS]

I. *3/4 tablespoon dry yeast (1 package)*
   1 1/2 cups lukewarm water
   1/4 cup sugar
   3 eggs, well beaten
   3 cups unbleached white flour

II. *1/2 cup oil*
   2 teaspoons salt
   2 to 3 cups whole wheat or unbleached white flour

Dissolve the yeast in the lukewarm water. Stir in the sugar, eggs, and unbleached white flour, and beat well. Cover and set aside to rise for 30 minutes. (For onion bagels, add 1 small, diced raw onion.)

Fold in the oil and salt. Then fold in the remaining flour 1/2 cup or so at a time until the dough comes away from the sides of the bowl. Turn out onto a floured board and knead for 5 minutes. Cover and let rise for 50 minutes. Punch down the dough and let rise another 30 minutes.

Cut the dough into thirds and shape each piece into a ball. (Cover the dough balls you are not working with a plastic bag or a moist towel to keep a crust from forming.) Cut the first ball into twelve pieces. Roll each piece into a tube, shape the tube around your first two fingers, and connect the ends together by rolling them beneath your fingers on the table.

After you have finished all twelve, dip each ring into boiling water for 10 seconds, to develop that genuine bagel crust.

Place the bagels on a greased cookie sheet, allowing them a little elbow room. Brush with Egg Wash (page 45) and sprinkle with sesame or poppy seeds, or leave plain. Let rise for 20 minutes.

Bake at 425° for 20 minutes or until golden brown.

Repeat the entire process with the second portion of dough. The third portion can be made into more bagels or a braided bread.

To make a braided bread, divide the dough into six portions. Roll each into a strand and braid (see the illustration for braiding six strands on page 60). Place on a greased sheet and let rise for 25 to 30 minutes. Brush with Egg Wash and sprinkle with poppy seeds. Bake at 375° for 45 to 50 minutes or until golden brown.

Muffins and Quick Breads

MUFFINS ARE WONDERFULLY QUICK AND EASY TO PREPARE, and generally they require only 20 minutes or so to bake. Plus, people are fond of muffins—at least I am.

Muffins are made by lightly combining wet ingredients—egg, milk, oil, and honey or molasses—with dry ingredients—flour, baking powder, salt. Mixing just until the dry ingredients are moistened (leaving a few lumps) will assure muffins of light, tender, even texture. Overmixing will make the muffins tough and chewy. Do not go there.

Quick breads are generally sweeter than muffins and intended more for desserts than as part of a meal. They are usually baked in loaf pans and are done when a toothpick or fork inserted in the center of the loaf comes out dry. Also, the bread will have begun to pull away from the sides of the pan and will be springy when pressed gently in the center.

A quick-bread batter may also be baked in muffin tins, with a reduced baking time. Muffin batters may be baked in bread pans, in which case the baking time is increased.

Jalapeño-Corn Bread

[SERVES 6 TO 8 PEOPLE]

This spoonbread is filled with the fresh flavor of corn accented with peppers or chilis — a hearty addition to a light meal. The milder (canned) green chilis may be used if jalapeños are not available or if you find them too hot. This bread is excellent served with Roasted Garlic and Hot Chili Butter (page 126).

2 tablespoons butter
1 cup white or yellow cornmeal
1 teaspoon salt
1 1/2 teaspoons baking soda
1 cup fresh corn with 1/2 cup cream stirred
   into it
3/4 cup milk
1/3 cup olive oil
3 eggs
1/3 cup roasted, peeled, and chopped jalapeño peppers or
   2 ounces canned minced green chilies
1 cup grated sharp cheddar or Monterey Jack
   cheese

Preheat oven to 400°.

Use a black 9-inch skillet or 1 1/2-quart earthenware casserole to melt the butter in a 400° oven. Meanwhile, combine the dry ingredients, then stir in the fresh corn, milk, oil, eggs, peppers, and half of the grated cheese. Remove the baking dish from the oven and pour the batter into it. Distribute the remaining cheese on top and bake for 35 minutes. Best served very hot.

VARIATION
To spice the bread up, add 1 teaspoon cayenne (or less! if the cayenne is very hot) to the dry ingredients.

This bread was invented quite by accident—by mistakenly adding more egg and milk than usual. One batter makes three layers. The cornmeal settles, the bran rises, in the middle is an egg-custardy layer. Easy, glorious, and amazing!

Three-Layer Corn Bread

1 cup cornmeal (coarse-ground works best)
1/2 cup whole wheat flour
1/2 cup unbleached white flour
1/4 cup wheat bran or wheat germ
2 teaspoons baking powder
1 teaspoon salt
2 eggs
1/4 to 1/2 cup honey or molasses
1/4 cup oil or melted butter
3 cups milk or buttermilk

Preheat oven to 350°.

Combine the dry ingredients. In a separate bowl, combine the wet ingredients. Mix together. The resulting batter will be quite liquidy.

Pour batter into a greased 9- by 9-inch pan. Bake for 50 minutes or until the top is springy when gently touched.

VARIATION
Add a cup of grated cheese—I like Monterey Jack, provolone, or Parmesan.

Corn-Sesame Breakfast Cake

[MAKES ONE
9-INCH CAKE]

This is a somewhat unusual recipe: a cornbread that is more of a cake with a crust on the bottom. It's a recipe that I adapted from the Turkish Coffee Cake Cookie Bars. You probably have not had very many things quite like it. Enjoy.

1 1/2 cups unbleached white flour
1 1/4 cups corn flour
1/2 cup brown sugar
1/4 cup white sugar
1 cup butter
1/2 cup sesame butter (or tahini)
1/4 cup honey
1 1/4 cups yogurt
1 egg
3/4 teaspoon baking soda

Preheat oven to 375°. Combine the flours and sugars, and cut in the butter until it is in tiny lumps. Press about half of this mixture (about 2 cups worth) into the bottom of a 9-inch cake pan (or perhaps an 8-inch-square baking pan). This will make the crust for the cake.

Combine the sesame butter, honey, yogurt, and egg. Mix the soda into the flour mixture, then the combined liquids. Pour into the pan on top of the pressed-down crust.

Bake for about 35 minutes until the center of the cake has risen and is bouncy to the touch. Or stick in a toothpick and see if it comes out clean.

Corn Muffins

SEE PAGE 108

Banana-Nut Bread

SEE PAGE 115

Honey Bars

SEE PAGE 132

Bartlett Pear Tart

SEE PAGE 159

Cinnamon Rolls

SEE PAGE 56

Cheesecake Cookies

SEE PAGE 130

Triple Chocolate Cake

SEE PAGE 149

Here is a basic whole wheat muffin recipe followed by a number of possible variations. Take your pick or dream up your own.

2 cups whole wheat flour
2 teaspoons baking powder
1/2 teaspoon salt
1 egg, beaten
1/4 cup oil or melted butter
1/4 to 1/2 cup honey or molasses
1 1/2 cups milk

Whole Wheat Muffins

[MAKES 12 LARGE MUFFINS]

Preheat oven to 400°.

Combine the dry ingredients. In a separate bowl combine the wet ingredients. Fold the wet and dry ingredients together with as few strokes as possible, *just until* the flour is moistened, leaving a few lumps. Spoon into greased muffin tins and bake for about 15 to 18 minutes.

A delicious whole wheat muffin, almost a cupcake.

1/2 teaspoon cinnamon
1/2 teaspoon mace
1/4 teaspoon nutmeg
1/4 teaspoon allspice
1/4 teaspoon ginger

Festival Spice Muffins

[MAKES 12 LARGE, FESTIVE MUFFINS]

Add these spices to the dry ingredients for Whole Wheat Muffins (above), and proceed with that recipe—being careful not to overmix!

Asian Spice Muffins

[MAKES
12 LARGE,
INSCRUTABLE
MUFFINS]

Another spiced-up muffin with exotic pretensions.

> 1/2 teaspoon cinnamon
> 1/2 teaspoon cardamom (best freshly ground)
> 1/4 teaspoon ground cloves
> 1/4 teaspoon freshly grated nutmeg
> 1/4 teaspoon ginger

Add these spices to the dry ingredients for Whole Wheat Muffins (page 105), and proceed with that recipe, being careful not to overmix.

Fruit Juice Muffins

[MAKES
12 LARGE,
STRANGELY
TINTED
MUFFINS]

Different colors and subtle flavors.

Use fruit juice in place of the milk in basic recipe for Whole Wheat Muffins (page 105) and proceed with that recipe. Other sweetening may be reduced or omitted. (For a really colorful effect, food coloring is necessary.)

Marmalade or Jam Muffins

[MAKES 12
LARGE, SUCCU-
LENT MUFFINS]

The marmalade or jam gives these muffins some unusual flavor variation.

Use 1/2 cup marmalade or jam in place of other sweetening in the basic recipe for Whole Wheat Muffins (page 105), and proceed with that recipe. (Do not overmix.)

The dried fruit makes these muffins chewy and sweet.

> *½ cup raisins*
> *or*
> *½ cup chopped dates*
> *or*
> *½ cup chopped dried apricots*

Make the recipe for Whole Wheat Muffins (page 105), adding one of the varieties of dried fruit above. (The dried fruit can be combined with the dry ingredients or the wet.) Avoid overmixing or the muffins will be tough.

Dried Fruit Muffins

[MAKES 12 LARGE, FRUITY MUFFINS]

The full, intense flavor of nuts or seeds enlivens these muffins.

> *½ to ¾ cup chopped walnuts*
> *or*
> *¼ to ¾ cup chopped almonds*
> *or*
> *½ to ¾ cup chopped cashews*
> *or*
> *½ to ¾ cup sunflower seeds*
> *or*
> *½ to ¾ cup roasted sesame seeds (roasted in oven*
> *   or frying pan)*

In addition to the regular ingredients in Whole Wheat Muffins (page 105), add any of the above. The nuts are more flavorful if lightly roasted before adding to the muffin batter. The sesame seeds, because they are so small, are difficult to chew, and roasting makes them easier to chew. Grinding them is another possibility. (Combine with the dry ingredients.) Proceed as in the basic recipe.

Nut or Seed Muffins

[MAKES 12 LARGE, NUTTY MUFFINS]

Confusion Muffins

[MAKES
12 LARGE,
FESTIVE,
INSCRUTABLE,
FRUITY, SUC-
CULENT, NUTTY
MUFFINS]

To go beyond the confines of the recipe may cause confusion or delight. Ready or not!

Combine any or all of the variations, or make up your own, and proceed as in the recipe for Whole Wheat Muffins (page 105) — being careful, in any case, not to overmix the wets and dries.

Corn Muffins

[MAKES 12
MUFFINS]

These are particularly adaptable to seasoning, so I have listed a number of options. The same batter can, of course, be baked in a pan for corn bread.

1 cup whole wheat flour
1 cup fine cornmeal
1/2 teaspoon salt
2 teaspoons baking powder
2 eggs, beaten
1/4 cup oil or melted butter
1 1/4 cups milk
1/2 teaspoon chili powder (optional)
1 teaspoon dry oregano (optional)
1 teaspoon dry marjoram (optional)

Preheat oven to 400°.

Combine dry ingredients, including your choice of the optional seasonings. Combine wet ingredients and then fold them together with the dry ingredients until just moistened. Spoon into greased muffin tins or a baking pan. Bake for about 15 minutes for muffins, about 25 minutes for corn bread.

Blue cornmeal comes from blue corn, grown in the Southwest by the Hopi, who talk and sing to each plant. If you come across some of this blue cornmeal, great, but the recipe can also be made with yellow or white cornmeal. And see what a difference it makes to talk and sing to each muffin. Your heart goes out to things, and things come home to your heart.

1 cup blue cornmeal
2 cups unbleached white flour
4 teaspoons baking powder
1/2 teaspoon salt
1/4 cup sugar
1 cup milk
3 eggs, well beaten
1/4 cup melted butter

Preheat oven to 400°.

Mix together the cornmeal, flour, baking powder, salt, and sugar. Combine the milk, eggs, and melted butter. Fold the dry ingredients into the wet until just barely moistened. Spoon into greased muffin tins and bake for 12 to 15 minutes or until lightly browned on top.

Blue Cornmeal Muffins

[MAKES 12 VERY LARGE OR 18 SMALLER MUFFINS]

Bran
Muffins

[MAKES 12
MEDIUM-TO-
LARGE BRANNY
MUFFINS]

These muffins have good bran flavor and a light and tender texture. They are good for snacks as well as breakfast. You may make the batter ahead of time, refrigerate, and bake muffins as you wish.

1 1/2 cups unprocessed wheat bran
1/2 cup boiling water
1 1/4 cups unbleached white or whole
    wheat flour
1 1/4 teaspoons baking soda
1/4 teaspoon salt
1/4 cup butter
1/2 cup sugar
1/4 cup molasses
2 eggs
1 cup buttermilk
3/4 cup raisins

Preheat oven to 400°.

Combine 1/2 cup of the bran with the boiling water and let it steep. Combine the remaining bran with the rest of the dry ingredients.

In a separate bowl cream the butter and sugar, then blend in the molasses and eggs.

Mix the steeped bran in with the buttermilk.

Add the dry ingredients to the butter-sugar mixture alternately with the buttermilk, beginning and ending with flour and mixing briefly after each addition.

Let the batter stand in the refrigerator for 12 hours. Spoon into greased muffin tins and bake for 18 to 25 minutes.

The batter will keep refrigerated up to 3 weeks.

These are moist and somewhat heavy but have a wonderfully nutty flavor. Definitely not as light as Wheat Flour Muffins.

Barley Flour Muffins

[MAKES 12 MUFFINS]

  2 cups barley flour
  2 teaspoons baking powder
  1/2 teaspoon salt
  1/4 cup honey
  2 cups milk
  1/4 cup oil
  1/2 teaspoon vanilla extract

Preheat oven to 400°.

Combine the dry ingredients. In a separate bowl combine the wet ingredients. Fold the dry and wet ingredients together, until the flour is just moistened. Spoon into oiled muffin tins. Bake for 20 minutes.

Is everybody a yuppie with their kitchen cupboard well stocked and fully supplied? I thought not. After much deliberation I finally decided to leave these recipes in the revised edition, so that, even with something missing, you can still make muffins. Some are more "muffiny" than others—the more they resemble the basic Whole Wheat Muffin recipe. Generally, muffins rise more when sweetened rather than unsweetened, when made with milk rather than water and with baking powder rather than without, with eggs rather than without.

Something Missing Muffins

A. SUBSTANTIAL MUFFINS

[MAKES 12 NOT LARGE BUT HEFTY MUFFINS]

  2 cups whole wheat flour
  1/2 teaspoon salt
  2 1/2 cups water or milk

Proceed as for Whole Wheat Muffins (page 105), being careful not to overmix.

[MAKES
12 HEAVY
MUFFINS]

B. STILL QUITE CHEWABLE

2 cups whole wheat flour
1/2 teaspoon salt
1/4 cup oil or melted butter
2 1/4 cups water or milk

Proceed as for Whole Wheat Muffins (page 105).

[MAKES 12
SOMEWHAT
TENDER
MUFFINS]

C. A SURPRISINGLY LIGHT MUFFIN WHEN MADE WITH MILK, BUT DON'T EXPECT TOO MUCH.

2 cups whole wheat flour
3/4 teaspoon salt
1/4 cup oil
1/4 cup honey or molasses
2 cups milk or water

Proceed as for Whole Wheat Muffins (page 105).

[MAKES 12
PRETTY GOOD,
NONPERFECT
MUFFINS]

D. ALL THAT'S MISSING IS THE EGG.

2 cups whole wheat flour
3/4 teaspoon salt
2 teaspoons baking powder
1/4 cup oil or melted butter
1/4 cup honey or molasses
2 cups milk or water

Proceed as for Whole Wheat Muffins (page 105).

Here is our bakery's version of an old standard: rich with butter, oil, and sugar; richly scented with cinnamon, allspice, and nutmeg; and richly filled with carrots, raisins, and nuts. Rich, rich, rich—yet it tastes so wholesome.

Carrot Cake

[ONE 10-INCH TUBE PAN OR TWO 8-INCH LAYER PANS]

1 cup white sugar
1 cup brown sugar
4 eggs
2/3 cup melted butter
2/3 cup oil
2 cups unbleached white or
*   whole wheat flour*
1 tablespoon cinnamon
2 teaspoons allspice
2 teaspoons freshly grated nutmeg
1 cup chopped walnuts
3 cups grated carrots
1 cup raisins (dark or golden)

Preheat oven to 350°.

Mix the two sugars and cream them with the eggs. Mix in the melted butter and oil. In a separate bowl, mix the flour, spices, and chopped nuts. Blend this mixture thoroughly into the sugar mixture. Stir in the carrots and raisins.

Put into a well-buttered and -floured 10-inch tube pan. Bake for 1 hour and 10 minutes. This cake may also be baked in two 8-inch layers. In this case, bake only for 30 to 35 minutes.

Let cake cool, and remove from the pan. Sift a little powdered sugar over it or crown it with Cream Cheese Icing (page 153).

Apple-Nut Loaf (Yeasted)

[MAKES 2 LARGE LOAVES]

Scented with vanilla, zested with orange peel, moist and fruity.

2 tablespoons yeast
1/2 cup sweet cider (lukewarm)
1 cup honey
1/2 cup oil
4 eggs, beaten
1/2 teaspoon salt
2 teaspoons vanilla extract
2 tablespoons finely chopped orange peel
4 cups whole wheat flour
4 cups grated raw apples with skins
1 cup coarsely chopped nuts (no peanuts)

OPTIONAL:
1 tablespoon cinnamon
1 teaspoon allspice

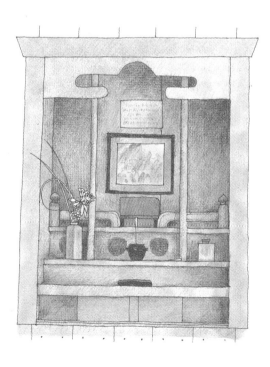

1 teaspoon nutmeg
1/2 cup coconut
1/2 cup dates or raisins

Preheat oven to 350° to 375°.

Soften the yeast in the cider. Blend together the honey, oil, eggs, salt, and flavorings. Add the yeast mixture, and then stir in the flour, apples, and nuts, as well as any of the optional ingredients.

Turn into oiled loaf pans. Let rise for 1 hour, and then bake for 45 to 60 minutes until nicely browned.

This bread has a higher proportion of banana pulp than most, which gives the bread a full banana flavor but also makes it a little less cakey. Good for dessert, it can also be toasted for breakfast.

2 cups whole wheat flour
1 teaspoon baking soda
1/4 teaspoon salt
1/2 cup butter or oil
1/2 cup sugar or honey
Grated rind of 1 lemon
2 eggs, beaten
2 cups banana pulp
1/2 cup chopped walnuts
1/2 cup raisins (optional)

Preheat oven to 350°.

Sift together the flour, soda, and salt. Cream the butter and sugar (or blend the oil and honey), then beat in the lemon peel and eggs. Add the sifted ingredients in three parts alternately with the banana pulp, beating smooth after each addition. Fold in the chopped nuts (and raisins if using them).

Banana-Nut Bread

[MAKES 1 LARGE LOAF]

Place the batter in a greased loaf pan and bake for about 50 minutes or until a toothpick inserted in the center comes out dry. Cool for 5 minutes before removing from the pan.

Honey-Walnut Bread

[MAKES 1 LARGE LOAF]

Milk and honey—there's nothing quite like it. Honey-Walnut Bread is fragrant and has a fine crumb.

1 cup milk
1 cup honey
1/2 cup soft butter
2 eggs, beaten
2 1/2 cups whole wheat flour (or 1/2 white and
   1/2 whole wheat)
1 teaspoon salt
1 tablespoon baking powder
1/2 to 3/4 cup chopped walnuts

Preheat oven to 325°.

Combine the milk and honey, and stir over low heat until blended. Remove from the heat and mix in the butter. When cooled to room temperature, beat in the eggs, flour, salt, and baking powder until well mixed. Fold in the nuts.

Place in a greased loaf pan, and bake for 1 hour or until a toothpick comes out clean. Cool for 15 minutes in the pan before removing. Let cool longer before slicing.

Date-Nut Bread

[MAKES 1 LARGE LOAF]

The recipe may call for whole wheat flour, but this bread is richly spiced and packed with dates and nuts.

2 cups whole wheat flour
2 teaspoons baking powder
2 teaspoons cinnamon

1/2 teaspoon mace
1/2 teaspoon salt
6 tablespoons butter
1/2 cup brown sugar
2 eggs, well beaten
1/2 cup milk
1 cup chopped dates
1/2 cup chopped walnuts
2 teaspoons grated orange peel

Preheat oven to 325°.

Sift together the flour, baking powder, spices, and salt. Cream the butter with the sugar, and beat in the eggs. Add the dry ingredients alternately with the milk, beginning and ending with the dry ingredients. Fold in the dates, nuts, and orange peel.

Place in a greased loaf pan, and bake for 1 hour or more until a toothpick comes out clean. Cool 5 minutes in the pan before removing to a wire rack. Serve plain or with butter or cream cheese. Delight in the simple good fortune.

Compound Butters

THIS SECTION WAS INSPIRED BY MY FRIEND SAMMIE Daniels, who had a catering business in Inverness, California. Presented here are only a few examples; as you can see, the possibilities are limited only by your imagination. So once you get started, you can experiment on your own.

The compound butters may be used any way you would use plain butter: on hot toast, muffins, pancakes; on bread or sandwiches; with vegetables or eggs.

Hidden flavors emerge. Delights are in store.

Nut Butters

Nut butters are adaptable to a great many uses, crossing all the boundaries from breakfast to dessert. In addition to being served with morning breads and pastries, they can be rolled up in pancakes with a little powdered sugar sprinkled on top: Almond and Orange Butter in Cottage Cheese Pancakes, for example.

They are excellent tossed with pastas or used as a garnish to perk up soups or steamed vegetables.

They can be served with quick breads: Almond and Orange Butter on Banana-Nut Bread or Apple-Nut Loaf, Hazelnut Butter on Honey-Walnut Bread, Pecan and Ginger Butter on Date-Nut Bread.

Or try these butters when making a dessert: Almond and Orange Butter used in making Apple Crisp or Hazelnut Butter in the Peach Kuchen. You get the idea. Or use the Pecan and Ginger Butter to enliven a fresh fruit tart, brushing it on the crust before adding the fresh fruit and glaze.

Hazelnut Butter

1/3 to 1/2 cup toasted and ground hazelnuts
1/2 cup sweet butter, softened
Splash of cognac

Roast the hazelnuts in a dry skillet over medium heat until fragrant and crunchy. Rub off and remove the skins that you can. Grind them in a coffee mill reserved for spices and nuts. Combine the ground nuts with the butter. Mix them very well and flavor with a splash of cognac. Roll into a log on waxed paper. Store tightly covered until ready to use.

Almond and Orange Butter

1/3 cup finely ground almonds or almond butter
1/2 cup sweet butter, softened
2 tablespoons freshly squeezed orange juice
Zest of same orange
1 teaspoon sugar
1 teaspoon rum (for zip)

Roast the almonds for 6 to 8 minutes in a dry skillet until fragrant and crunchy. Chop lightly, then grind more completely in a coffee mill reserved for nuts and spices. Mix the almonds with the butter, and then little by little work in the orange juice, zest, sugar, and rum. Pack into a 1-cup ramekin and store covered in the refrigerator.

Pecan and Ginger Butter

1/2 cup very finely ground pecans
1/2 cup sweet butter, softened
1 1/2 tablespoons very finely minced crystallized ginger or
    2 teaspoons grated fresh ginger or 1 teaspoon dry ginger
1 teaspoon brown sugar (optional)
1/2 teaspoon allspice (optional)

Roast the pecans in a dry skillet over medium heat until fragrant and crunchy. Grind in a coffee mill reserved for nuts and spices. Mix the pecans with the butter, and stir in the ginger. After tasting, see if you'd like sugar and allspice, more ginger, or both (or it's just fine, thank you). Chill in a ramekin. Keeps at cool room temperature.

Sweet Butters

Try these sweet butters in the morning with toast, muffins, bagels, or breakfast rolls. Heap Chocolate Nutmeg Butter on toasted Country French Bread, or Coffee Liqueur Butter on a Flaky Biscuit. How about Honey Lemon Butter on Lemon Twist Bread or Vanilla Bean Butter on Cream Scones?

Honey-Lemon Butter

1/2 cup sweet butter, softened
2 tablespoons honey
Juice and zest of 1 medium lemon

Combine all the ingredients and stir well with a fork. Form into a log on waxed paper or chill in a butter mold until ready to use. Well wrapped, this keeps for a week or longer in the refrigerator.

Chocolate-Nutmeg Butter

1/2 cup sweet butter, softened
3 tablespoons sweetened cocoa
1/2 whole nutmeg, grated

Combine all the ingredients in a small bowl and mix well. Form into a log and roll in waxed paper. Chill until hard, then unwrap and cut into bite-sized pieces.

Vanilla Bean Butter

1/2 cup sweet butter, softened

2 vanilla beans, soaked in hot water for
    20 minutes

3 to 4 tablespoons sifted powdered sugar
    or more to taste

In a small bowl, combine the butter and the scrapings only from the vanilla beans. Mix well and sift in the powdered sugar. Chill in a pretty mold and serve on a plate.

Coffee Liqueur Butter

1/2 cup sweet butter, softened

2 tablespoons instant coffee powder

2 tablespoons Kahlúa or coffee liqueur

Powdered sugar to taste

In a small bowl, combine the butter and coffee powder. Blend in the liqueur and some sifted sugar to taste. Form into a log on waxed paper or put into a mold. Chill.

Savory Butters

The savory butters, like the nut butters, are versatile: use them to accompany breads, garnish soups, and flavor vegetables or pasta dishes. Spread on little toasts, they can be used to garnish and float in a bowl of soup. Try the Roasted Garlic and Hot Chili Butter on the Jalapeño-Corn Bread. The Lemon-Mustard Butter is always great on a sandwich. The Lime and Cilantro Butter is wonderful on tortillas or with Corn Muffins. The Balsamic Butter is delicious spread on rye bread.

Balsamic Butter

4 tablespoons balsamic vinegar
2 tablespoons red wine
6 tablespoons sweet butter
Salt
Pepper

In a saucepan, combine the vinegar and wine and reduce by half. Beat in the butter 1 tablespoon at a time until a thick emulsion develops. Season with salt and pepper. Serve warm, or chill in a small dish and use like cold butter.

Lemon-Mustard Butter

1/2 cup sweet butter, softened
1 1/2 tablespoons Dijon mustard
1 to 2 tablespoons fresh lemon juice
Salt
White pepper

With a fork, cream together the butter, mustard, and lemon juice. Taste; then add some salt and pepper. Shape into a log on a piece of waxed paper or clear plastic. Wrap and chill. When hard, cut into 1/4-inch pieces to serve.

Lime and Cilantro Butter

3/4 cup sweet butter, softened
Juice and zest of one lime
1/2 cup chopped fresh cilantro
Salt
Pepper

In a small bowl, combine the butter, lime juice and zest, and cilantro, then season to taste with the salt and pepper. Form into a log on waxed paper or plastic or put into a butter mold. Chill until ready to use, then cut off small pieces and arrange on a plate.

Roasted Garlic and Hot Chili Butter

3/4 cup salted butter, softened
3 cloves garlic, oven-roasted in their skins until quite soft
1 1/2 teaspoons red pepper flakes
Salt to taste

Place the butter in a small bowl. Squeeze the cooked garlic cloves from their skins and mash well into the butter, adding the red pepper to taste. Add a little salt as necessary. Roll into a log on a piece of waxed paper. Chill until hard. Serve on anything you want to spice up. Good in soups, too.

Desserts

A GOOD DESSERT MAKES A CELEBRATION OF ANY OCCASION. Not that we have to treat ourselves royally every day, but offering dessert with generosity and warmth, we can appreciate the bounty of our lives and celebrate a moment of aliveness. How sweet it is.

Once upon a time we were not really into desserts, were we? We put up with them, begrudgingly or at a distance. Sugar, we said, rots the body and mind. Well, times change. We have stopped depriving ourselves of real desserts and congratulating ourselves for our forbearance. No sugar, no enlightenment.

Now, I do not mean to encourage people to become sugar junkies, and I myself cannot eat sugar at the rate I used to and still function with clarity and alertness. But I am also not going to scold people for eating a dessert that is really a dessert. Every moment is a gateway to the truth. Which way is in? Which way is out? Are you entering or leaving?

So the long and short of it is that this section of the book has greatly expanded from the first edition. I have added several recipes from our Tassajara Bread Bakery in San Francisco, including Chocolate Mousse Pie and Triple Chocolate Cake, as well as some other very pleasant cookies and cakes. Still included are the squares and bars from the original *Bread Book*, which offer the advantage of being less time-consuming than the cookies which need to be individually shaped. The round and circular of cookies truly gratifies and pleases, but when you do not have the time, make a panful of cookie, get out your knife, and do the cutting.

May all beings be healthy, happy, free from suffering.

And may desserts celebrate our wondrous nature. Fully.

Cheesecake Cookies

[MAKES 16
2-INCH-SQUARE
COOKIES]

I've always loved these cookies, as they are beautiful and quick to make. Cut into squares, triangles, or diamonds, they easily serve large numbers of people.

1 cup whole wheat flour

1/3 cup brown sugar

1/3 cup butter

1/2 cup chopped walnuts or toasted sesame seeds
  or roasted sunflower seeds

8 ounces cream cheese

1/4 cup honey

1 egg

2 tablespoons milk

1 tablespoon lemon juice

1 tablespoon grated lemon peel

1/2 teaspoon vanilla extract

1/4 teaspoon freshly grated nutmeg (optional)

GARNISH (OPTIONAL):
Fruit slices: orange, apple, banana, apricots,
  strawberries or other berries
Nutmeats (whole or chopped): almonds, walnuts, Brazil nuts

Preheat oven to 350°.

Blend together the flour, sugar, and butter with a pastry cutter to make a crumbly texture, then mix in the 1/2 cup chopped walnuts. Reserve 1/2 cup of the mixture for the topping, and press the remainder into an 8-inch square pan. Bake at 350° for 12 to 15 minutes.

In the meantime soften the cream cheese and blend in the honey, egg, milk, lemon juice and peel, and seasonings. Spread over the baked crust and sprinkle on the reserved topping. Garnish, if you wish, with fruit slices and/or nutmeats — if you know how you plan to cut it later, you can put one fruit or nut on each piece. Bake for 25 minutes. Cool and cut into 2-inch squares.

Note: If using strawberries or other berries for a decorative garnish, put them on the cheesecake after baking—the colors and flavors will be brighter and fresher.

Here is another of my old favorites, quick to make and delicious to eat. Chocolate chips (or fruit slices) can be put between the layers if you like.

Turkish Coffee Cake Cookie Bars

[MAKES 24 1½- BY 3-INCH BARS]

> 2 cups whole wheat flour
> 1 cup brown sugar
> 2 tablespoons Turkish-type coffee or powdered
>   instant coffee
> 2 teaspoons cinnamon
> ½ teaspoon freshly grated nutmeg
> ¼ teaspoon allspice or ground coriander
>   (optional)
> ½ cup butter
> 1 cup sour cream
> 1 egg, beaten
> 1 teaspoon baking soda
> ½ cup chopped nuts
> 4 ounces chocolate chips (optional)

Preheat oven to 350°.

Mix together the flour, sugar, coffee, and spices, then cut in the butter with a pastry cutter until crumbly. Press half of this mixture into a 9- by 13-inch pan. Mix the remaining half with the sour cream, egg, soda, and chopped nuts. If using chocolate chips, sprinkle them over the crust in the pan. Pour the batter on top of the crust. Bake for 25 to 30 minutes, until the middle is springy.

I've also made this with apple or pear slices between the layers of crust on the bottom and cake on the top.

Honey Bars

[MAKES ABOUT
24 LARGE
BARS]

Soft but chewy, these bars are fragrant with an exquisite bouquet of spices, honey, and fruit peel. Robust and hearty rather than delicate and airy, they can be kept for several weeks in a tightly closed tin.

1 1/2 cups honey

3 tablespoons butter

2 cups whole wheat flour, sifted with 1 tablespoon
    baking powder

2 tablespoons chopped lemon or orange peel or
    1 tablespoon of each

2 teaspoons cinnamon

1/2 teaspoon freshly ground cardamom

1/4 teaspoon ground cloves

1/4 teaspoon mace or allspice or ground coriander
    (optional)

1/2 cup chopped almonds or other nuts

1 1/2 to 2 cups whole wheat flour

Preheat oven to 350°.

Have all the ingredients ready to mix quickly before the mixture stiffens with cooling.

Heat the honey in a saucepan slowly just until liquidy; remove from the heat. Stir in the butter and then the sifted flour with baking powder to make a thick batter. Add the fruit peel, spices, and nuts, and then add the additional flour until a dough forms.

Pat the dough into a buttered pan — 9 by 13 inch is good (or you can use a portion of a baking sheet) — until you have a layer 3/8 inch thick. Bake for about 20 to 25 minutes. Be careful not to overbake or the cookies will be quite hard. When done, the bottoms will be lightly browned and the tops dry but not browned. (If you end up with hard cookies, dip in tea or coffee as you would biscotti.) Remove from the pan while still warm and slice into bars. Then cool before storing.

VARIATION

To make more of a "fruitcake" honey bar, add 1/4 cup each of chopped citron and chopped candied orange or chopped lemon peel along with the spices and nuts.

These can be whipped up in just a few minutes and eaten in about the same length of time or lingered over indefinitely. Raisins, figs, or prunes can be substituted for dates.

Date Bars

[MAKES 18 TO 24 BARS]

3 eggs
1/2 cup brown sugar
1 teaspoon vanilla extract
1 cup whole wheat flour
1 teaspoon baking powder
1/8 teaspoon salt
1/2 teaspoon ground cloves
1 teaspoon cinnamon
1/2 teaspoon allspice
1 cup chopped dates or raisins
*   or figs or prunes*
1/2 cup chopped nutmeats

Preheat oven to 325°.

Beat eggs until light. Gradually blend in the brown sugar along with the vanilla. Sift together the flour, baking powder, salt, and spices, add them to the eggs, and beat until well blended. Fold in the fruit and nutmeats. Pour into a buttered and floured 9- by 13-inch pan and bake for 20 to 25 minutes.

Tassajara Shortbread

This shortbread may be quickly pressed into the bottom of a tart pan or made into cookies. These light, little cookies can be topped with pecan halves or dipped in chocolate. Simple, but delightful.

> *1 cup salted butter*
> *1/2 cup powdered sugar*
> *2 cups unbleached white flour*
> *Splash of vanilla extract*

Preheat oven to 350°.

Cream together the butter and sugar. Mix in the flour and perhaps a little vanilla. Press into the bottom of a 10-inch tart pan with removable sides. Bake for 25 to 30 minutes. Remove from the oven, cut into squares (or wedges) while still hot, and allow to cool. This shortbread will keep for several weeks in a tin.

VARIATIONS

• To make the shortbread into cookies, roll the dough into a log about 2 inches in diameter. Wrap in waxed paper or plastic and refrigerate for 20 to 30 minutes before slicing into cookies. Place on an ungreased cookie sheet and bake at 350° for about 20 minutes.

- For pecan shortbreads, place a pecan half on each cookie before baking.
- For chocolate shortbreads, dip the top of the already-baked cookies in melted bittersweet or semisweet chocolate or in one of the chocolate glazes (page 150).

Uncommonly lemony, simple, and quick to prepare, these lemon bars provide a crisp tartness in a refreshing, light dessert — one of those desserts that I find *so* good, as in "where have you been all my life?"

Lemon Bars

FOR THE SHORTBREAD CRUST:
1 1/4 cups flour
1/4 cup sugar
2/3 cup butter, chilled and cut into 1/2-tablespoon pieces

Preheat oven to 325°.

To prepare the crust, work the flour, sugar, and butter together until they form a dough. Press this into an 8-inch round or square pan. Bake for 20 minutes.

FOR THE LEMON FILLING:
2/3 cup sugar
2 teaspoons baking powder
1/2 cup fresh lemon juice
2 eggs
Zest of 1 lemon

Prepare the filling while the shortbread is baking. Whisk together the sugar, baking powder, lemon juice, and eggs along with the zest. Pour this mixture over the baked crust and continue baking another 30 minutes or until slightly browned on top. After it cools, sift a little powdered sugar on top, if you like. Cut into squares.

Italian Cookies

[MAKES APPROXIMATELY 30 COOKIES]

Scented but not too sweet, dryish and crunchy but not too tough, these cookies are great for coffee-dipping or tea-dunking.

1 cup sweet butter
2 cups sugar
2 eggs
4 cups unbleached white flour
2 teaspoons baking powder
2 teaspoons anise extract
1 1/3 tablespoons orange extract

Preheat oven to 350°.

Cream together the butter and sugar. Beat in the eggs. Then mix in the flour and baking powder. Add the anise and orange extracts and blend thoroughly. Divide the dough into four equal pieces, shape into flat-bottomed logs, and put two each on well-greased baking sheets. Bake until a toothpick comes out clean. Baking time varies with the thickness of the logs. Check them after 30 minutes. Cut the logs while still warm into 1/2-inch pieces and let them cool completely. They keep well in a tin.

Walnut Cookies

[MAKES APPROXIMATELY 18 COOKIES]

Delicate, airy, melt-in-your-mouth, these cookies may get consumed before making it out of the kitchen.

2 1/4 cups unbleached white flour
1 cup softened butter
1/3 cup brown sugar
1 teaspoon vanilla extract
2/3 cup finely chopped walnuts
Powdered sugar

Preheat oven to 350°.

Reserve ¼ cup of the flour and then combine all ingredients in the order listed. Add the reserved flour as necessary until the dough comes away from the sides of the bowl.

Form into balls 1½ inches in diameter and place on a well-greased baking sheet 2 inches apart.

Bake until firm to the touch, about 20 minutes. After baking, the cookies may be tossed in powdered sugar.

The original *Bread Book* did not have a single cookie recipe. Sure, there were bars and squares, but no cookies: I never had time to make them. To shape individual cookies for fifty or eighty people can take a while, so I made sheet pans of desserts which I could cut into serving-sized pieces.

Since then, I have rediscovered cookies, and I have found this one to be a wonderful, ethereal cookie, which simply melts in your mouth. I could not believe how good these were the first time I tried them. I am sure to bake some around the holidays.

Chocolate-Walnut Cookies

[MAKES 3 DOZEN OR MORE COOKIES]

3/4 cup sweet butter, softened
1/2 cup white sugar
1 egg
4 ounces unsweetened baking chocolate, melted and cooled
2 teaspoons vanilla extract
1 cup finely ground walnuts
1 teaspoon baking powder
2 1/4 cups unbleached white flour

Preheat oven to 350°.

I usually just dump everything into the bowl and mush it together with my hands, but if you want . . .

Cream the butter and blend in the sugar. Mix in the egg, beating well, then the chocolate, vanilla, and nuts. Combine the baking powder with the flour, then mix into the other ingredients. The dough should be dry enough to shape into balls with your hands without too much sticking to your fingers, and wet enough that it does not crumble apart. If necessary, add more flour to make it drier. Add a spot of water or a bit more butter to moisten. Roll the dough into balls the size of walnuts and place on an ungreased cookie sheet, leaving about 2 inches in between. Press them flat with a cookie stamp, a glass, or a teacup. Flour the bottom of the pressing implement if it sticks to the cookies. Bake for 8 minutes. They are done when the tops of the cookies are cracked, and the bottom slightly browned.

Coconut Macaroons

[MAKES 12 LARGE COOKIES]

Intensely sweet and coconutty, these macaroons can satisfy any sweet tooth, especially when they are dipped in chocolate, as in the variation. This recipe utilizes egg whites only, so if you need to use some yolks, you can add them to the Lemon Bars or use them in the Vanilla Pastry Cream, page 152.

1/2 cup egg whites (probably 3 eggs)
Pinch of salt
1 1/2 cups sugar
3/4 teaspoon vanilla extract
3/4 teaspoon almond extract
2 tablespoons flour
14 ounces dry, unsweetened coconut (shredded)

Preheat oven to 300° to 325°.

Beat egg whites with salt until soft peaks form. Gradually add the sugar, continuing to beat until stiff. Beat in vanilla and almond extracts. Fold in flour and coconut until thoroughly incorporated.

Drop very large spoonfuls at least 2 inches apart, onto a greased baking sheet.

Bake until firm and slightly golden. Remove the macaroons from the sheet while still hot and cool them on a rack.

VARIATION

For chocolate coconut macaroons: Melt 2 ounces of bittersweet chocolate over a slow flame and stir until melted. Dip the bottoms of the macaroons in the melted chocolate and turn upside down to dry.

Revised to work! These cookies are crunchy with cornmeal, millet meal, bread crumbs, nuts, and seeds. They are not particularly stylish or sweet, but are full of good old grit and wholesome country flavors.

Nutty Gritty Cookies

[MAKES A BUNCH]

1/2 cup oil
1/2 cup honey
2 cups bread crumbs (or 1/2 cup
  whole wheat flour)
1 1/2 teaspoons salt
1 cup sesame seeds, roasted (dry-roast
  in pan or oven)
1 cup sunflower seeds, roasted
1 cup rolled oats, lightly roasted
1 cup walnuts, lightly roasted, chopped
1 cup cracked millet
1 cup fine cornmeal
1 cup raisins
Water as needed

Preheat oven to 350°.

Blend the oil and honey together, then mix in the remaining ingredients except for the water. Add water a little at a time until the mixture holds together. If the mixture gets too wet, add some more flour. Shape into balls and place on a lightly oiled cookie sheet. Bake for about 25 minutes.

Haver Cookies

[MAKES ABOUT 24]

One of our no-sugar, no-honey classics, this recipe makes a chewy but not tough "cookie"—or perhaps better called a "cracker." A good, wholesome snack food with excellent grain flavors.

1/2 cup currants or raisins
1 1/4 cups rolled oats
2 teaspoons cinnamon
1/2 teaspoon salt
2 tablespoons corn oil
1/2 cup whole wheat flour
1/2 cup unbleached white flour
5 to 7 tablespoons apple juice

Preheat oven to 350°.

Soak raisins in water for 30 minutes. Combine oats, cinnamon, and salt. Add oil, stir thoroughly, and set aside. Mix flours and juice. Add the oat mixture and then the drained raisins. If the mixture does not hold together, add extra teaspoons of oil or juice until it does.

Shape the mixture into a ball and place it on a large greased baking sheet. Roll the dough with a heavy rolling pin into a large rectangle 1/4 inch thick. Using a sharp knife, cut across the dough to form rectangular strips 3 to 4 inches wide. Then cut zigzag fashion across each rectangle to form triangles.

Bake the Havers for 20 to 30 minutes. Do not brown. Let cool and remove from the pan. Store in a tin.

This is an unusual cake, made without eggs, baking powder, sugar, or honey. The texture is dense yet soft and crumbly. I have not tried this with flours other than wheat, but they would probably work fairly well (for those with wheat allergies). Surprisingly delicious.

1 cup oil
1 cup nut pieces, chopped (almond, walnut, pecan,
   hazelnut)
1 cup raisins
1 cup coconut
2 cups rolled oats
3 cups crushed fruit (pulp and juice)
1/2 teaspoon salt
1 teaspoon vanilla extract
2 to 2 1/2 cups whole wheat flour

Preheat oven to 350°.

For the crushed fruit, use strawberries, other berries, pineapple, banana, apricot, peaches, nectarines. The fruit may be coarsely chopped or blended to a puree. Apples or pears may also be used if first cooked and made into sauce, or grated with juice added for liquid.

Mix together all the ingredients except for the wheat flour. Then add the flour to form a soft, slightly crumbly dough. The amount of flour will vary with the moisture content of the fruit.

Press or spread into buttered pans (about 1/2-inch thick) and bake for 40 to 50 minutes until the sides and bottom are golden brown. (Take a peek.) Let cool in the pans for 10 minutes before turning out onto a plate or board for further cooling. Frost with a date filling, decorated with pieces of fresh fruit.

To make the date filling, place 1/2 pound pitted dates in a saucepan with water to cover and simmer for 10 to 15 minutes until the dates are soft. Mash into a paste or whip in a blender, and season with lemon or orange peel.

Fresh Fruit Cake

[MAKES 2 9-INCH ROUNDS]

Sesame Candy (Halvah)

To make this homemade halvah you will need some way to grind the sesame seeds—most practical is probably an electric coffee mill reserved for nuts, seeds, and spices. After that, it is simple to sweeten and spice.

2 cups unhulled sesame seeds
1 tablespoon sesame oil (optional)
1/4 cup or more honey or sugar
2 tablespoons butter or tahini

SPICES (OPTIONAL, TO TASTE):
1 teaspoon vanilla extract
1/4 teaspoon cloves
1/2 teaspoon cinnamon
1/4 teaspoon cardamom or coriander or nutmeg or mace
Whole roasted sesame seeds, for coating (optional)

Roast the seeds until they are crunchy—in a frying pan over a moderate flame or on a baking sheet in the oven (8 minutes at 350°). Stir often enough that they roast evenly. Grind the seeds finely, but not so finely that you end up with sesame butter. Add the sweetening and the butter (and the sesame oil if using it). Taste. The basic recipe is not very sweet, so you may well wish to add more honey or sugar and some vanilla. If you want the halvah to have some spiciness, take your pick of the spices and season to taste. Shape into balls and roll in toasted sesame seeds, or press onto a cookie sheet and refrigerate before slicing into pieces.

Raw Fruit-Carob Candy

Still trying to be good and not eat chocolate? Or do you just really love the flavor of carob? Here is a way to enjoy carob without sugar or oils.

2 cups pitted dates
1 cup seedless raisins

¹/₂ cup chopped walnuts (optional)
Carob powder
¹/₂ cup sesame seeds, toasted

Grind the dates and raisins together or chop them to a coarse paste. Add the walnuts if using them. Add as much carob powder as the mixture will hold. Shape into balls and roll the balls in roasted sesame seeds.

VARIATION

Mix 1 cup of roasted, ground sesame seeds with the dates and raisins before adding the carob powder (sesame halvah carob date raisin candy coming up).

Here is a simple recipe for a light dessert or tea treat.

1 pound of cream cheese at room temperature
³/₄ cup raisins or chopped dates
Whole wheat flour
¹/₂ cup grated dry unsweetened coconut
1 tablespoon grated lemon or orange rind
¹/₂ teaspoon allspice
³/₄ cup chopped almonds or sesame seeds or
*   sunflower seeds*

Cream
Cheese
Balls

[MAKES 16 TO 24]

Soften the cream cheese. If using dates, mix them with a small amount of whole wheat flour to separate. Blend the raisins or dates, coconut, fruit peel, and allspice in with the cream cheese. Squeeze everything together in your hands and shape into 1-inch balls. Roll the balls in the chopped almonds or toasted seeds.

Apple Crisp

[SERVES 6
PEOPLE]

The antecedents of this apple crisp go back to the Saturday night bar becues before Tassajara was bought by the Zen Center. Tossed salad, half chickens, pork ribs, French bread, baked potatoes, green beans, corn on the cob, red and white wine — wouldn't that get you ready for apple crisp with vanilla ice cream?

4 to 6 pippin apples
Juice of 1 lemon
1 teaspoon or more cinnamon
1/2 teaspoon or more freshly grated
    nutmeg
1/2 to 3/4 cup brown sugar
1 cup whole wheat flour
Pinch of salt
1/2 cup unsalted butter
Whipped cream, and lots of it

Preheat oven to 375°.

Wash, quarter, core, and slice the apples, thickly or thinly. Toss with the lemon juice and then arrange in a buttered 9- by 13-inch pan. Sprinkle on the cinnamon and freshly grated nutmeg. Mix the sugar, flour, and salt together and cut in the butter with a pastry cutter until it is in pea-sized lumps. Sprinkle this topping onto the apples.

Bake for about 45 minutes or until the apples are fork-soft.

Serve plain or topped with whipped cream and a grating of nutmeg. Ice cream will also do — nicely.

VARIATION

The crisp can also be made with peaches, pears, nectarines, or apricots. Dabbling with other spices is also permitted, though a light hand is advisable — or you'll just be tasting the spice and not the fruit.

A peach-jeweled mosaic set in custard baked on a sweet crust. My next-door neighbor Jennifer makes an awesome version of this dessert with pears from her backyard Superfina pear tree.

Peach Kuchen

[SERVES 2 TO
12 PEOPLE
(DID THEY
EAT DINNER
FIRST?)]

> 2 cups flour
> 1/4 teaspoon baking powder
> 1/2 teaspoon salt
> 1 cup brown sugar
> 1/2 cup butter
> 12 skinned peach halves or 2 packages frozen peach slices
>   (or other fruit)
> 1 teaspoon cinnamon
> 2 egg yolks, beaten, or 2 whole eggs
> 1 cup heavy cream or sour cream

Preheat oven to 400°.

Note: To remove the skins from fresh peaches, dip them in boiling water for 10 to 15 seconds and then peel. If the peaches are not so ripe and the skins are hard to remove, the peaches can be left longer in the boiling water.

Combine flour, baking powder, salt, and 2 tablespoons of the sugar. Cut the butter into the flour mixture with a pastry cutter until it looks like coarse meal. Press this firmly into a baking pan (9 by 13 inches is probably about right). Arrange the peach halves on the surface. Mix the remaining sugar with the cinnamon and sprinkle it over the fruit.

Bake for 15 minutes, then beat the yolks together with the cream and pour it over the top, and bake an additional 40 minutes at 375° or until the peaches are soft and the custard has thickened.

VARIATION
Use other fruits—pears, as I mention above, are especially good. Apricots or nectarines would also work well.

Torte with Sour Cream Fruit Topping

[SERVES 6 OR MORE PEOPLE]

A wonderfully soft, velvety texture (enhanced with the cornstarch), scented with vanilla and mace, makes this an excellent cake to absorb the juices of the fruit and sour cream. This recipe could also be used for strawberry shortcake.

1/2 teaspoon mace
1 teaspoon vanilla extract
1/2 cup butter
1 cup white sugar
1 cup sifted white flour
1/2 cup cornstarch
1 1/2 teaspoons baking powder
1/2 teaspoon salt
2 large eggs, beaten
1/4 cup milk

Preheat oven to 350°.

Blend the mace and vanilla into the butter. Cream in the sugar. Sift together the flour, cornstarch, baking powder, and salt. Beat the eggs and milk together. Add the dry ingredients to the butter-sugar mixture alternately with the eggs and milk, beginning and ending with the dry ingredients. Mix well after each addition.

Butter and flour a 9-inch cake pan. Add the batter and bake for 45 minutes or until the center is dry. Cool in the pan for 20 minutes, then turn out onto wire rack. Turn right side up.

FOR THE TOPPING:
2 to 3 tablespoons honey or sugar
1 cup sour cream
1/2 teaspoon vanilla extract
1 to 2 cups (sliced) fruit

Combine topping ingredients and mix in fruit pieces of the season's choosing.

This fine-crumbed, melt-in-the-mouth cake is beautiful served in slices on a large platter with powdered sugar sprinkled over them. It also may be served with fruit and whipped cream, or even toasted for breakfast.

Yogurt Cake

[SERVES 12 PEOPLE]

1 cup unsalted butter

2 cups sugar

5 egg yolks

3 cups cake flour, sifted with 1 1/2 teaspoons baking
*   powder and 1/4 teaspoon mace*

1 cup yogurt

5 egg whites

1/2 cup sugar

1/4 teaspoon salt

1/4 teaspoon cream of tartar

Preheat oven to 350°.

Cream the butter and sugar until fluffy. Beat in the yolks one at a time. Add the flour mixture alternately with the yogurt, beginning and ending with flour.

Beat the egg whites until they form soft peaks, gradually adding the sugar, salt, and cream of tartar.

Fold half of the whites into the batter — and then fold in the remaining half. Bake in a greased and floured tube pan for 50 to 60 minutes. Test with a toothpick. If it comes out clean, the cake is done.

VARIATION
This cake like the Torte above is excellent with fresh fruit pieces — or in the winter stewed dried fruit.

Mustard Gingerbread

I think of gingerbread as a ho-hum sort of dessert, until I bite into a forkful. The real thing is incomparably better than the thought. Here are some directions that could turn into that real-thing gingerbread — with your helping hand.

> 2 1/4 cups sifted whole wheat flour
> 1 1/2 teaspoons baking powder
> 1/2 teaspoon salt
> 1/2 teaspoon baking soda
> 1/2 teaspoon cloves
> 1 teaspoon powdered mustard
> 1 teaspoon cinnamon
> 1 teaspoon powdered ginger
> 1/2 cup butter
> 1 cup molasses
> 1 large egg
> 1 cup hot water
> Whipped cream

Preheat oven to 350°.

Sift together the flour, baking powder, and salt. Blend the soda and spices into the butter. Gradually blend in the molasses, followed by the egg. Add the flour mixture alternately with the hot water, beginning and ending with the flour and mixing thoroughly after each addition.

Turn into a buttered-and-floured 9-inch square pan or a loaf pan and bake for 45 to 50 minutes or until a toothpick comes out clean from the center. Cool in the pan for 10 minutes before turning out to finish cooling. Serve with whipped cream (or applesauce or peach slices).

Intense chocolate flavor and melt-in-the-mouth texture make this cake a delicious and satisfying chocolate dessert. Both the cake and the icing are only moderately sweet.

Triple Chocolate Cake

[MAKES 1 9- TO 10-INCH CAKE]

>   *5 ounces semisweet chocolate*
>   *1 1/2 ounces unsweetened chocolate*
>   *3/4 cup butter*
>   *1/2 cup white sugar*
>   *4 egg yolks*
>   *1/2 cup cake flour or unbleached white flour*
>   *1/2 cup ground almonds*
>   *4 egg whites*
>   *1/8 teaspoon cream of tartar*
>   *1/4 cup white sugar*

Preheat oven to 375°.

Melt chocolates and butter over a very low flame or in a double boiler. Once the chocolate and butter begin to soften, stir until smooth, remove from heat, and set aside to cool.

Beat 1/2 cup sugar into the yolks until light and lemony in color. Beat in the somewhat cooled chocolate mixture. Stir in the flour and almonds until the flour is dissolved.

Beat the egg whites with the cream of tartar until soft peaks form, then beat in 1/4 cup sugar a little at a time until the whites are stiff. Fold one-third of the whites into the batter to lighten it, then carefully fold in the remaining whites so as to maintain as much volume as possible.

To prepare the pan, first butter it, then cut out a sheet of waxed paper to fit the bottom. Butter the waxed paper and dust with flour. Pour the batter into the pan and smooth out the surface.

Bake the cake in the middle third of the oven for 50 minutes or until the edges have pulled away from the sides and the middle of the cake is springy. Let cool in the pan for 10 minutes and then remove to a rack. When cooled, it may be left plain or iced with Simple Chocolate Glaze (below).

Simple Chocolate Glaze

[GLAZES A 9- TO 10-INCH LAYER]

This icing does not mound up but is thick enough to nicely glaze the Triple Chocolate Cake (page 149) or another of your choice.

6 ounces semisweet chocolate
3/4 cup butter at room temperature
Flavoring (optional): vanilla, brandy, rum, or
   Grand Marnier

Melt the chocolate slowly in a double boiler. Remove from heat and work in the butter a little at a time until blended. Add flavoring if desired. Let cool to room temperature before icing the cake.

Chocolate Glaze

[ENOUGH FOR 2 MEDIUM LAYERS OR I LARGE CAKE]

An easy-to-prepare glaze that will elegantly *choclify* any cake or cookie.

4 ounces bittersweet chocolate
3 tablespoons sugar
3 tablespoons water
3 tablespoons sweet butter

Grate or break up the chocolate and put it in a heavy saucepan with the sugar and the water. Melt slowly over very low heat or in a double boiler. Stir until the chocolate is barely melted, and remove from heat. Stir in the butter 1 tablespoon at a time, until the mixture is satiny-smooth.

Let the glaze continue to cool and thicken to a spreading consistency. Pour over the cake and let it drip down the sides.

I know everybody likes chocolate, but I like vanilla, too, so here is a dessert that utilizes both.

> *½ cup butter, softened*
> *¾ cup sugar*
> *2 eggs*
> *1 teaspoon vanilla extract*
> *1½ cups unbleached white flour*
> *2 tablespoons dry milk*
> *2½ teaspoons baking powder*
> *⅝ cup water*

Preheat oven to 350°.

Cream the butter, then cream in the sugar. Add the eggs one at a time—along with the vanilla—and beat well to blend. Combine dry ingredients. Stir in the dry ingredients alternately with the water, beginning and ending with the dry.

Grease and flour two 8-inch round layer pans and divide the batter between them. Bake for 20 minutes until golden on top. Let cool in the pans for a few minutes before removing to a cooling rack.

This may be assembled with Vanilla Pastry Cream (page 152) between the layers and Buttercream Frosting (page 152) on top.

For Boston Cream Pie: Put Vanilla Pastry Cream (page 152) between layers and one of the chocolate glazes (page 150) on top.

Vanilla Pastry Cream

This pastry cream can be used between layers of cakes or underneath fresh fruit in a tart. In the sense that it utilizes cornstarch, this is not a classic pastry cream, but it's dependable and you don't need to watch it so closely.

2 tablespoons plus 1 teaspoon cornstarch
1 cup milk
3 egg yolks
1/3 cup sugar
1 tablespoon cream
1/2 teaspoon vanilla extract

Dissolve cornstarch in a couple of tablespoons of the milk. In a separate bowl, beat the yolks, then whisk in the rest of the milk, the sugar, cream, and vanilla. Heat in a double boiler while whisking. When the mixture begins to steam, add the cornstarch solution. Whisk continuously until well thickened to mayonnaise consistency. Remove from pan and let cool before refrigerating. Chill before using.

Other flavorings may also be used.

Buttercream Frosting

[ENOUGH TO LAYER AND TOP AN 8-INCH CAKE]

A very buttery, very creamy-smooth frosting, one we used to use at our bakery. It works well for decorating and can be flavored in a variety of ways. This recipe is a lot of work without a mixer.

3 egg whites
1 cup sugar
2 tablespoons corn syrup
5/8 cup sweet butter, softened
Flavoring: vanilla extract, Kahlúa, or Grand Marnier

Blend egg whites, sugar, and corn syrup together, and put in a double boiler to heat. Meanwhile, whip the butter until it is "white 'n' light." Heat the whites until they are too hot to touch and the sugar granules have dissolved. Then remove them from the heat and whip them until they turn marshmallow. While continuing to whip the whites, add the whipped butter a handful at a time. Season with vanilla, Kahlúa, Grand Marnier, or other liqueur, or try a spot of lemon juice. Use immediately or keep refrigerated.

We have used this on our Carrot Cake and other cakes. White and creamy, it also can be used for cake decorating.

Cream Cheese Icing

[ICING FOR 1 LARGE CAKE]

> *8 ounces fresh cream cheese at room temperature*
> *1/2 cup sweet butter at room temperature*
> *3 cups powdered sugar*
> *1 teaspoon vanilla extract*
> *Juice and zest of 1/2 lemon*

Cream together the cream cheese and butter. Slowly sift in the powdered sugar and beat until the mixture is well blended and has no lumps. Then stir in the vanilla and lemon.

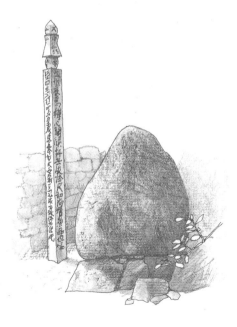

Chocolate Mousse Pie

A dessert classic, chocolate mousse, juxtaposed with a chocolate crust, the creamy smoothness of the filling given a bed of crunchiness. Irresistible for chocolate-lovers. The recipe calls for making up a double batch of chocolate "cookies" which are to be made into crumbs for the pie shell. The double batch makes enough crumbs for two shells, so you will have some crumbs on hand for next time. Although it may look complicated, this mousse pie is surprisingly easy to prepare. Note: In place of the chocolate crust, you could also use (one of) the Short Pastry for Tarts, page 156 (or buy some chocolate cookies to crush).

FOR 2 PIE SHELLS:
2 ounces unsweetened chocolate
1/4 cup butter
1/2 cup sugar
1 egg
1 teaspoon vanilla extract
1 teaspoon milk
1 1/2 cups unbleached white flour
3/4 teaspoon baking powder
1/4 teaspoon baking soda
Pinch of salt
1/4 cup melted butter per pie shell

To prepare the pie shell:

Preheat oven to 325°. Melt and stir the chocolate and butter over very low heat or in a double boiler. Remove from heat when melted. Pour into a bowl. Mix in the sugar, then blend in the egg, vanilla, and milk. Stir in the flour, along with the baking powder, soda, and salt.

Spread batter about 1/4 inch thick on a greased baking sheet. Bake for 25 minutes. Remove from the oven and break into pieces about 1-inch square. Continue baking another 15 minutes. Let cool. Make the pieces into crumbs by placing them in a ziplock plastic bag and crumbling them with a rolling pin. This makes enough crumbs for two pies.

For each pie (about 1½ cups of crumbs), mix in ¼ cup of melted butter. (If you are making just one pie, store the other half of the crumbs in a closed container.) Press the buttered crumbs by hand into a 9-inch pie tin, evenly distributing them on the sides and bottom.

FOR EACH MOUSSE FILLING:
8 ounces semisweet chocolate
2 egg yolks
2 egg whites
1 whole egg
¼ cup sugar
1 cup whipping cream
¼ cup rum

To prepare the mousse filling and assemble the pie:

Melt the chocolate over a very low flame or in a double boiler. Heat slowly, just enough to melt, stirring some to help it along. Remove from heat. Separate two eggs. Combine the yolks with the whole egg. Beat the egg whites to soft peaks, then add the sugar and continue beating until stiff but not dry. In a separate bowl, whip the cream and add the rum to it. Whisk the egg and yolks and mix in the chocolate. Fold in the whipped cream one-third at a time. Fold in the whites. Fill the pie shell and smooth off the top. Refrigerate.

The pie may be decorated with rosettes of whipped cream if you have a pastry tube.

Short Pastry for Tarts

[MAKES I LARGE CRUST]

Here are two recipes for tart crust, which can be used for Fresh Fruit Tarts, as a substitute for the chocolate crust in Chocolate Mousse Pie, or as a crust for other pastries of your choosing.

1 1/2 cups unbleached white flour
1/4 cup white sugar
Pinch of salt, or to taste
3/4 cup sweet butter
2 egg yolks
1 1/2 teaspoons vanilla extract
2 teaspoons cold water

Sift the dry ingredients together, and work in the butter (with a pastry cutter) until the mixture resembles corn meal. Stir in the yolks, vanilla, and water, and form the dough into a ball, working briefly with your hands just until the flour is all incorporated. Wrap in plastic and chill thoroughly—at least 30 minutes.

[MAKES I CRUST]

Here is the other one, and then the directions for baking.

1 1/2 cups unbleached white flour
2 tablespoons powdered sugar
1/4 cup finely ground almonds
Pinch of salt, or to taste
1/2 cup sweet butter, cut into small pieces
1 egg
2 tablespoons lemon juice (or water)

Preheat oven to 400°.

Combine the flour, sugar, almonds, and salt. Cut the butter into the dry mixture with a pastry cutter until it becomes mealy. Add the egg and lemon juice or water. Work together until the flour disappears and the dough no longer sticks to your hands. Place in a plastic bag and form into a ball and then into a disk 6 to 8 inches in diameter. Chill for at least 30 minutes.

To prepare the crust:

Remove the dough from the refrigerator and roll it out to fit an 8- to 10-inch tart pan with a removable bottom. Place the dough in the pan, press it into the edges, and fill in any tears or gaps with some of the overlap. Prick all over with a fork. Cover with foil and line the foil with dried beans or peas. Bake for 10 minutes and then remove the foil and beans. Use this for a partially baked shell, or return to the oven another 8 to 10 minutes to finish baking to a light golden brown.

Glazed fresh fruit on a thin layer of Vanilla Pastry Cream set in a tart shell: jewellike, luscious, creamy, sweet, buttery — I find fresh fruit tarts beautiful, delicious, and intensely satisfying. Another piece, please.

Fresh Fruit Tart

Short Pastry for Tarts (page 156)
Vanilla Pastry Cream (page 152)
Fresh fruit (enough to layer the tart)
Fruit jam

Make one of the Short Pastries and bake it to a light golden brown. Remove from the oven and let cool.

In the meantime, make up a batch of Vanilla Pastry Cream. Spread a layer of pastry cream over the bottom of the tart — about 1/4 inch thick. (You will not need a whole batch of pastry cream; leftovers can be kept refrigerated.)

Arrange fresh fruit on top of the pastry cream. Berries are probably the best (soft, colorful, and flavorful) for this: strawberries, blueberries, raspberries, ollaliberries, blackberries. Kiwi, peeled and sliced, is excellent, as well as banana — diagonal slices are pretty. Peaches and nectarines need to be quite ripe (and the peaches peeled), then the fruit sliced. Seedless grapes can be part of the design. Apricots and pitted cherries flash with color and flavor. Thinly sliced cross sections of orange are refreshing. You are on your own for selection and design. Some fruits are generally too hard to be used uncooked, but if you are imaginative you can try apples or pears.

To glaze the fruit: gently heat some fruit jam or preserves (of the same, similar, or contrasting fruit) until it is runny, season with lemon juice, and brush it over the fruit. Ready to appreciate and enjoy.

VARIATIONS

- A simpler fruit tart can be made by brushing the heated jam or preserves on the baked tart crust, arranging the fresh fruit, and topping with more glaze.
- Or line the bottom of a baked crust with sour cream flavored with vanilla and sweetened with sugar or honey. Then top with fruit and glaze. Cream cheese can also be used to line the tart shell, thinned with milk or sour cream, sweetened with sugar or honey, flavored with vanilla and/or lemon peel or juice. Then arrange the fresh fruit on top and brush with the glaze.

Fresh Fruit Cheesecake Tart

This recipe is good with fruits that can take some baking: apples, pears, apricots, peaches, possibly nectarines. Some of the berries are OK too, if you like them really soft. (You get the idea that I prefer the Fresh Fruit Tart for berries?)

[MAKES 1 TART]

1 tart shell, partially baked (see Short Pastry for Tarts, page 156)
4 ounces cream cheese
2 tablespoons honey or sugar
1 egg
1/4 cup sour cream or 2 tablespoons milk
1/4 teaspoon vanilla extract
Grated peel of 1/2 lemon
Fresh fruit (enough to layer the tart)
Fruit jam or preserves (apricot or raspberry are good if you cannot decide)

Preheat oven to 350°.

Make up and partially bake a Short Pastry for Tarts.

Meanwhile, soften the cream cheese with a mixing spoon, then blend in the sweetening, the egg, and then the sour cream or milk. Mix in the seasoning.

Pour the cream cheese mixture into the partially baked tart shell. Arrange the fresh fruit decoratively on top of the cream cheese. If using apples or pears, slice them thinly, and arrange in a slightly overlapping pattern. Apricots can be left halved. Peaches (and possibly) nectarines are probably best peeled. (Plunge in boiling water for 10 to 15 seconds before peeling to loosen the skins.)

Heat some fruit jam or preserves (using the same, similar, or contrasting fruit) over a low flame until liquidy. Brush it on top of the fruit. Bake the tart for 20 to 25 minutes or until the fruit has softened and the cream cheese has firmed. Remove from the oven and repeat the glazing if you wish.

Bartlett Pear Tart

[SERVES 4 TO 6 (OR EVEN 8) PEOPLE. MAKES ONE 9-INCH TART]

Tarts by their nature tend to be more decorative than pies. I always buy the pears a few days in advance to give them time to ripen. I've done this various ways, but here is today's. It is made with a crumb topping underneath the pears to soak up their juices. Of course, other types of pears than Bartletts can also be used to make the tart. I especially enjoy the Comice and Seckel pears from my yard.

Tart Dough (see below)
2 tablespoons sweet butter
2 tablespoons white sugar
1/4 cup white flour
1/8 teaspoon cardamom
1/8 teaspoon anise seeds
2 to 3 red Bartlett pears

Preheat oven to 375° to 400°.

Make up the tart dough (or crumble) below and press it into a 9-inch tart pan (with a removeable bottom), starting with the edges and then filling in the middle. Be careful to press into the *corners* of the pan so that the dough is not too thick there. Cut the butter and sugar into the flour along with the spices. Distribute over the tart dough.

Quarter the pears, core, and then cut into diagonal slices. Arrange decoratively in the tart pan, fanning them out or placing them in concentric circles, skin side up, starting from the outside . . . or . . . you figure it out. If you wish, sprinkle just a little sugar on top.

Bake for about 35 to 40 minutes until the sides of the tart are nicely browned and the pears are tender.

[FOR ONE
9-INCH
TART]

TART DOUGH:

1/4 cup whole wheat flour
1 cup white flour
2 tablespoons sugar
1 teaspoon grated lemon peel
1/2 cup sweet butter
1 teaspoon vanilla extract
1 tablespoon water

Combine the flours with the sugar and the lemon peel. Cut in the butter until it is in pea-sized pieces. Add the vanilla extract and water and mix in lightly. Although this is called a dough, it does not really need to come together in a piece, as it will be pressed into the tart pan. Keep it on the dry side.

ABOUT THE AUTHOR

WRITING ABOUT MYSELF IS PRETTY DIFFICULT, AS MUCH OF it can be blurbs and clichés, which reveal little. The proof's in the pudding, isn't it? Taste me in the bread—and your good-hearted effort.

First coming to Tassajara when it was still a resort, in May 1966, I got a job as the dishwasher, learned to make bread, soups, and scrub the floor. I could never understand the cooks losing their temper. Then one of the cooks quit. Offered his job, I jumped right in over my head. Instantly I understood—in fact I acquired—cook's temperament. What a shock! You know you're in trouble when they start having meetings to discuss what to do with you.

During that summer my friend Alan and I did zazen together. One time Suzuki Roshi came down with several students, and we sat together in cabin 3B. "The first thing to do in setting up camp is to carry water and gather wood. Now we have carried water and gathered wood," he said.

The next spring I was suddenly head cook of a monastery, as the Zen Center had purchased the property. Twenty-two years old and about as sure of my position as a leaf which falls in the winter creek. Proceeded to do a lot of things which I didn't know how to do, learning firsthand, the blind leading the blind. Bumped my head quite a bit, and a few other people's heads also. The actual cooking, I discovered, was the easiest part of the job. I was head cook at Tassajara for three summers and two winters, until, being completely devoured, bones cast aside, I was exhausted of food.

For a while I built stone walls, which was not such heavy work after all—and sifted rocks out of the dirt in the lower garden.

Moving to the Zen Center in San Francisco, I was guest manager, head of the meditation hall, head resident teacher, president, chairman of the board. (A strange business: going to the mountains to attain true realization, only to become an executive officer in a huge *corporation*.) At Greens, our restaurant in San Francisco (beginning in 1979), I was busboy, dishwasher, waiter, host, cashier, floor manager, wine buyer, manager (everything but cook). At home I have been married, divorced, coupled, uncoupled, father of a daughter (great blessing).

Leaving the Zen Center in 1984, I moved to a cabin in the bay trees in Inverness, California, and over the next twenty years worked on four books, and began teaching cooking, baking, and meditation, nationally and in Europe. After being an institutionalized person for twenty years (at the Zen Center), I found it extremely challenging to earn a living, buy groceries, pay bills, figure out taxes, and drive in traffic. Friends would sympathize by saying, "If you hadn't already done it, I would suggest you go to a Zen monastery for a while." It took about ten years to stop telling myself that I should just drop everything and go back to Tassajara.

Through all the years after Zen Center, I have continued to cook and bake. It's a choice I keep making: to honor and bless by preparing food to share.

I can be reached through my website, www.peacefulseasangha.com, or by writing to me c/o Shambhala Publications, 300 Massachusetts Avenue, Boston, Massachusetts 02115.

ABOUT TASSAJARA

TASSAJARA IS AN ISOLATED, NARROW VALLEY AT THE END of a fourteen-mile dirt road that winds three thousand feet up into the mountains and three thousand feet down. The road passes madrone, buckeye, oak, pine, ferns, brush, manzanita, yucca, and, at the crest along the ridge, looks east to the Salinas Valley, west to the Coast Range. Along here, there are evenings when the full moon is rising in the east while the sun sets in the west. The light of the sun and moon accentuate the ruggedness and wide-ranging quality of the mountains. Driving the road takes fifty to sixty minutes — passing places with precipitous drop-offs of hundreds of feet — so when you get to Tassajara, you feel relieved to have arrived somewhere at last.

News does not always reach here right away. No television, no radios; newspapers are usually at least a day old, if not a week. Big news comes by phone if the phone is working and if somebody hears it ringing and answers it. Formerly a single wire strung from tree to tree made the connection — most of the time, and now a radio phone does the same.

Tassajara is site of Zen Mountain Center, a Zen Buddhist meditation center, open to visitors in the summer. Zen Center of San Francisco purchased Tassajara in December of 1966. What had been the bar became the meditation hall (for a number of years until it burned down in 1978).

The autumn, winter, and spring months are a time of solitude, of retreat, with thirty to fifty residents, and no visitors. Residents, while following a schedule of meditation, study, and work, are seeking the Way: the way to live fully, the way to untangle the tangle within and without, the way to realize and express the deepest truth in everyday ways — perhaps by baking! In summer months, May through Labor Day, we open our gate to visitors, accommodating the public with overnight facilities and three family-style vegetarian meals daily. We cook for seventy to eighty guests and sixty or more students daily. We have been at it since the summer of 1967.

Guests, having traveled the long road, find themselves remote and distant from the anxieties and turmoil of the daily grind. Free to make their own schedule, they can relax and let be, enjoy the sun and water, the swimming pool and swimming hole downstream, the hot baths and steam rooms upstream. A hot springs resort since the 1880s, Tassajara's baths utilize water preheated nature's way deep underground. Surfacing through fissures, collected in catch basins and a holding tank, the water is finally piped to the baths. Luxurious. No need here to do, to accomplish, to produce — it is enough to walk, to read, to breathe easily and rest assured, and, of course, to eat.

For our guests we want to cook something special, something delicious, something to dream about. A variety of homemade breads provide sustenance at most lunches, while biscuits, pancakes, coffee cakes, scones, and muffins contribute to breakfasts. Cookies at lunch, desserts at dinner — the day is replete with bakery items. And each summer guests purchase a thousand loaves of bread to take home.

What makes our food special is what goes into the cooking. What goes into our cooking is generosity more than genius, kindness more than sophistication. We labor. Our food tends toward *rustic* or *country* rather than *chic* or *city*. What makes food — and everything else — special is the everyday caring, considerate effort. We work this way not for pay but because we choose to offer our best effort. Engaging, awakening activity springs up, is summoned, called forth, invited — the guests are waiting.

None of our staff is professional, including the cooks and bakers. We do not live and work here to make a living, but to fulfill our lives. We have been drawn to the mountains, drawn to meditation, drawn to a life we create and share together. Tassajara is a peaceful place, a safe place to unwind, to "take off the blinders, and unpack the saddlebags," to make oneself at home with oneself. Settling into the depths. Falling right through the depths. Awakening in the moment. How is it, after all?

Each summer a new group of students arrives to practice meditation and works to take care of the guest season. You're invited to join in.

Tassajara can be reached through the San Francisco Zen Center website, www.sfzc.org, or by writing to Tassajara, 39171 Tassajara Road, Carmel Valley, California 93924.

INDEX